An Ever Present Danger:
A *Concise History of British Military Operations on the North-West Frontier, 1849-1947*

Matt M. Matthews

Occasional Paper 33

Combat Studies Institute Press
US Army Combined Arms Center
Fort Leavenworth, Kansas

Library of Congress Cataloging-in-Publication Data

Matthews, Matt, 1959-
  An ever present danger: a concise history of British military operations
on the North-West Frontier, 1849-1947 / Matt M. Matthews.
      p. cm.
  ISBN 978-0-9841901-3-3
  1. North-West Frontier Province (Pakistan)--History, Military--19th
century. 2. North-West Frontier Province (Pakistan)--History, Military--
20th century. 3. Great Britain. Army--Colonial forces--Pakistan--North-
West Frontier Province--History--19th century. 4. Great Britain. Army--
Colonial forces--Pakistan--North-West Frontier Province--History--20th
century. 5. Pashtuns--Pakistan--North-West Frontier Province--History-
-19th century. 6. Pashtuns--Pakistan--North-West Frontier Province--
History--20th century. 7. Afghan Wars. I. Title.

  DS392.N67M38 2010
  954.91'2035--dc22
                              2010017048

First Printing: June 2010

Contents

Maps

Introduction

> When you find yourself fighting in frontier warfare, you
> open the old British manuals. You will find they contain
> many lessons.
>
> Lieutenant General Asad Durrani
> Pakistani Army, 2009

Recent Pakistani military operations against the Taliban have once again thrust the historically volatile region of Pakistan's North-West Frontier into the international limelight. According to a number of Pakistani military officers, the current fighting bears a striking resemblance to operations conducted by the British in the North-West Frontier during its long and bloody history of conflict with the frontier Pashtun ("Pathan" as the British dubbed them) tribes. [1] Going through the old imperial gazetteers, Pakistani Major General Athar Abbas pointed out in 2009; "You see ambushes are taking place in exactly the same locations now as they were in the 1890s. The people of the frontier have always been fierce fighters and their motivation has remained the same, whether they are fighting the British, the Soviets, or a Pakistan government supported by the Americans. As they see it, they are fighting occupation."[2]

Indeed many Pakistani Army officers are examining the official histories of British military operations and the numerous manuals, instruction booklets and unofficial works by British officers addressing their thoughts on fighting in the North-West Frontier and Afghanistan. Possibly one of the most recognized unofficial published works of the twentieth century is General Sir Andrew Skeen's *Passing It On: Short Talks on Tribal Fighting on the North-West Frontier of India*, which was published in 1932. In the preface to his book, Skeen noted; "When young, I once had cause to thank a senior for his wise teaching of the needs of frontier fighting. His reply was; 'That's all right youngster, pass it on.' I acted on it during the rest of my service and am doing it now in the only way left to me."[3] By 1939, Skeen's small volume was in its fourth edition. Certainly Skeen and a myriad of other British and Indian soldiers who served in the North-West Frontier have a good deal to "pass along" to more modern armies, including members of the Coalition forces, that are currently operating in this same frontier region against an enemy called the Taliban.

Interestingly, the Taliban and other extremist organizations in the border region belong almost exclusively to the trans-border Pashtun tribes. As Thomas H. Johnson and M. Chris Mason have pointed out; "The implications of the salient fact that most of Pakistan's and Afghanistan's violent religious extremism and with it much of the United States' counterterrorism challenge, are centered within a single ethnolinguistic group, have not yet been fully grasped by a governmental policy community that has long down-played cultural dynamics."[4] Given the magnitude of the current situation in the trans-border region, it is surprising that little historic analysis has been conducted on the nearly 100 year history of British military operations against the Pashtun tribes of the North-West Frontier.

In what would surely prove a prophetic piece of advice, the preface to the British Army's official history of the 1920–1935 campaigns on the North-West Frontier, which was published in 1945, surmised that; "Wars between 1st Class Modern powers come and go. Armaments and battlegrounds change with each upheaval. The tribes of the North-West Frontier of India however, remain as heretofore an unsolved problem. The Indian Army of the future will still have to deal with the Mohmands and Afridis, Mahsuds and Wazirs. History repeats itself. Let it be read profitably."[5] Certainly, the US Army and its partners can benefit from a historical study of British military operations on the North-West Frontier.

It should be understood, however, that the British Army in India never performed anything resembling modern counterinsurgency (COIN) operations against the Pashtuns. Rather, for the most part, the British sought not to exert enduring political authority over the Pashtun tribes along the frontier but to maintain tribal autonomy and friendly relations with those groups in order to maintain stability in the region. For the British, the wellbeing of its colony in India was the main objective and maintenance of peace along the North-West Frontier was a means of achieving that goal. For long periods of time, British Imperial policy was one of non-interference and many tribesmen were enthusiastically accepted into the ranks of imperial military forces. Punitive military operations were often carried out only after tribesmen committed a crime or conducted a raid outside the tribal region. The goal was to punish the errant tribesmen promptly by destroying villages, crops and livestock, and killing the fighters and scattering the traditional Pashtun fighting forces which were called *lashkars*. The British objective was to swiftly inflict pain on the tribes and bring them to terms. Still, the British campaigns along the frontier relied heavily on tactical innovations focused on defeating an elusive enemy that used unconventional operations along the lines of the Taliban. This threat required a succession of British leaders to introduce tactical innovations, which included new forms of maneuver and the integration of indigenous Pashtun personnel into the ranks of its forces. This study will focus on these elements as the means of providing the most relevant insights for US Army units and other Coalition forces active in the region today.

The accumulated knowledge and experience gained by British and Indian forces in Frontier Warfare provides a host of important tactical lessons for the US Army. The British found early on that their Field Service Regulations required considerable alterations when conducting operations against the trans-border tribes of the North-West Frontier. For example, the introduction to the British *Manual of Operations on the North-West Frontier of India*, which was published in 1925 concluded; "The modifications referred to in this manual are such as experience has shown to be necessary in operating against such an enemy as is met with on the North-West Frontier of India and the instructions are intended to supplement, not supersede, those contained in Field Service Regulations and the training manuals of the various arms."[6]

The British Army in India soon learned that the Pashtuns made excellent soldiers. As early as 1845, a veteran British officer published an unofficial work intended to teach young officers how to train and command these native soldiers. For many years, Pashtuns serving in the imperial ranks performed valiantly and efficiently. However, on more than one occasion, the British found to their dismay that the Pashtun officers and soldiers they had trained so effectively had no misgivings about applying their newfound martial skills against the army that had taught them.

While attempts to "pass on" the experience of training indigenous Pashtun forces or preserve other important lessons of frontier warfare frequently proved beneficial, the British often paid a heavy price in casualties and equipment when this tactical and administrative knowledge was not properly retained or was ignored by soldiers in the field. Oftentimes, soldiers lacking solid basic training found that they were no match for the clever and highly motivated Pashtun guerilla forces. Finally, and perhaps most importantly, while the British typically achieved tactical successes, they habitually ended each operation with a strategic withdrawal. As British historian Alan Warren observed, "On each occasion the tribes in the mountains won a strategic victory, despite local tactical reverses, and the bulk of the Indian Army's troops were forced to withdraw back onto the plains of the Indus Valley."[7]

This Occasional Paper will examine the almost continual efforts of British and Indian soldiers (both regular and irregular) to combat and pacify the Pashtun tribes of the North-West Frontier. It will also examine the tactics employed in the various campaigns. Chapter 1 deals briefly with the historical background of the British in India, geography of the North-

West Frontier, the Pashtun tribes, and a short account of the First Afghan War. Chapter 2 addresses British military operations from 1849–1900 and discusses the Punjab Irregular Force (PIF) and its efforts to stop Pashtun raids into Punjab, as well as early punitive expeditions into the North-West Frontier. The chapter also examines the failure to pass along the lessons of the PIF to the British and Indian regular forces as they deployed for the first time in strength into the North-West Frontier during the Pashtun revolt of 1897. The chapter additionally investigates the renewed tactical effectiveness of the Pashtun tribes, brought about by modern and more effective weapons. Chapter 3 will explore British attempts to capture the lessons of the 1897–1898 Pashtun revolt by publishing new training manuals, instituting new training programs, and folding the irregular forces into the British and Indian Regular Army. The chapter will examine the success of these programs (the 1908 *Khel* and *Mohmand* campaigns), and the dire consequences of their abandonment prior to the 1919–1921 *Waziristan* Campaign. Chapter 4 will examine the challenges confronting the British and Indian Army on the North-West Frontier during the 1920s and 1930s. The chapter will discuss British attempts to "Pass It On" or incorporate the past lessons of "hill warfare." The results of these new tactical adjustments will be explored by examining the 1935 *Mohmand* campaign, the 1936–1937 *Waziristan* campaign, and British efforts to track down and kill the elusive *Faqir* of *Ipi*. The final chapter will offer an analysis of lessons learned by the British on the North-West Frontier and their relevance for the US Army and its allies.

Notes

1.   The author will use the term Pashtun throughout the text to refer to the main ethnic group on the North-West Frontier and the Pakistan-Afghanistan border region. When quoting from other sources, the terms Pashtun and Pathan will be used interchangeably.

2.   David Rose, "Hunting the Taliban in the footsteps of Winston Churchill: On lawless battlefields nothing has changed in a century," *Daily Mail Online*, 20 June 2009, http://www.dailymail.co.uk/news/worldnews/article-1194352/Hunting-Taliban-footsteps-Winston-Churchill.html (accessed 21 June 2009).

3.   General Sir Andrew Skeen, *Passing It On: Short Talks On Tribal Fighting on the North-West Frontier of India* (London: Gale and Polden, 1932); T.R. Moreman, *The Army in India and the Development of Frontier Warfare, 1849–1947* (London: Macmillan Press Ltd., 1998), 240.

4.   Thomas H. Johnson and M. Chris Mason, "No Sign until the Burst of Fire: Understanding the Pakistan-Afghanistan Frontier," *International Security*, Vol. 32, No. 4 (Spring 2008), 42.

5.   *Official History of Operations on the North-West Frontier of India 1920–1935* (Sussex, UK: Published jointly by The Naval & Military Press Ltd. and The Imperial War Museum, n.d.), vii; quoted in T.R. Moreman, 183–184.

6.   *Manual of Operations on the North-West Frontier of India* (Calcutta, India: Government of India, Central Publication Branch, 1925), 1.

7.   Alan Warren, *Waziristan, the Faqir of Ipi and the Indian Army: The North-West Frontier Revolt of 1936–1937* (Oxford, UK: Oxford University Press, 2000), 290.

Map 1. Map Depicting Pashtun Majority Area.

Chapter 1

The Pashtuns and The First Afghan War

We are content with discord, we are content with alarms, we are content with blood. We will never be content with a master.

Elderly Pashtun Tribesman, 1809

The conceit of Imperial Britain to assume that its forces were vastly superior to any other native army east of the Suez would more than once prove disastrous but this was the most egregious miscalculation of all.

John H. Waller
Beyond The Khyber Pass

Background

By 1818, The East India Company, under the auspices of the British government, was firmly entrenched in India. Driven by colonial ambition, the Company had managed by the 1830s to increase its assets, expanding north to the border of Nepal and in the east, to the edge of Burma. Only in the west was the Company's expansionist policy stymied by the imposing military forces of the Punjab. However, with the death of the powerful ruler of Punjab, Ranjit Singh in 1839, the British began casting their gaze towards the lands west of the Indus River, specifically Afghanistan. Many within the British Government believed the distant kingdom would make an excellent "buffer" to counter Russian encroachment from the north.[1]

Geography and the Pashtuns

Sandwiched between the ill-defined border of Afghanistan and Punjab, lies a lengthy expanse of territory known as the North-West Frontier. This harsh and mountainous terrain was inhabited by various independent Pashtun tribes who were linked by the Pashtu language and other cultural connections to their brethren in Afghanistan. In fact, many of the tribes were trans-border clans inhabiting areas on both sides of the indistinct boundary. Composed of approximately 350 tribes, each containing numerous clans or *khels*, the Pashtuns are the largest ethnic group within the North-West Frontier. According to one expert in the field, the individual tribesman was:

> Surrounded by concentric rings consisting of family, extended family, clan, tribe, confederacy, and the major cultural-linguistic group. The hierarchy of loyalties cor-

respond to these circles and become more intense as the circle gets smaller. Seldom does the Afghan, regardless of cultural background, need the services and/or the facilities of the national government. Thus in the case of crisis, his recourse is to kinship and, if necessary, the larger cultural group. National feelings and loyalties are filtered through the successive layers.[2]

For centuries, the inhospitable terrain and the autonomous warrior ethos of the Pashtuns allowed them to resist all outside rule or authority. David Dichter writes; "Because of the craggy wilderness of their mountains, the Pathans have been able to remain free of the troublesome external authority of social institutions in a way that is almost unprecedented in the history of either the eastern or western world."[3] The Pashtuns are a fiercely democratic and independent people and while most or all are Sunni Muslims, their distinct and unwritten code of *Pashtunwali* is the true foundation and guiding principle of their society. As an example, an erstwhile Pashtun proverb declared; "Obey the mullah's teachings but do not go by what he does."[4]

Pashtunwali, which means "the way of the Pashtun," is sacred within their culture. "The more one adheres to its maxims," wrote the renowned Pashtun authority, Sher Muhammad Mohmand, "the more high esteem he enjoys in his brotherhood and community."[5] The code, according to Mohmand, compels Pashtuns; "to defend their motherland, to grant asylum to fugitives irrespective of their creed or caste and to offer protection even to his deadly enemy and to wipe out insult with insult."[6] As a result, revenge plays a key role in *Pashtunwali* with reprisals often being repaid tenfold. Today, little has changed. In a recent article in *The New York Times*, Ganesh Sitaraman declared that; "In the midst of these interconnected insurgent relationships, tribal feuds and blood feuds between families put the Hatfields and McCoys to shame."[7] One Pashtun, wrote Sitaraman, "waited 40 years before taking vengeance on his neighbor. Insurgency was his cover for retribution."[8]

This unremitting cycle of vengeance often kept the Pashtun tribes at each other's throats, and as a result, they were often incapable of uniting under a unified banner. On the other hand, if their homeland was threatened or a *Faqir* or Mullah could incite the tribes into a jihad (holy war) against the foreign infidel, the Pashtuns were capable of uniting for brief periods against a perceived enemy. When the drums beat, the tribes would form into a *lashkar* which is a term usually applied to a warrior force of over 200 men. Mohmand pointed out that; "*Lashkar* as used in the tribal sense, can

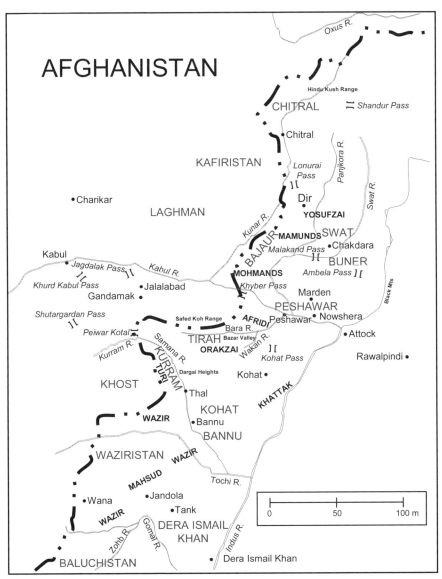

Map 2. The Pashtun Tribes. Tribal names in Bold Script.

be employed as a crusade or a holy war or can even be against a particular policy of the government. The tribal *lashkar* in the latter case continues until the political authorities see it appropriate to sit down with them across the table and carve out an amicable settlement."[9] It would prove a Pashtu term that the British would come to know well.

The North-West Frontier is slightly over 700 miles, with widths varying between 60 and 280 miles. This combines an unwelcoming landscape with an equally unreceptive tribal society.[10] In the far north at Chitral, the Hindu Kush Mountains dominated the landscape. South of Chitral, in Dir Swat, the Yusufzai tribes occupied the productive valleys inter-spaced between the 15,000 to 22,000 feet high mountains. Southwest of Swat, the Mohmand tribes straddled the border north of the strategically important Khyber Pass. South of the Khyber Pass and Peshawar, the Afridi tribes occupied the area. In the Tirah region, south of the Afridi tribes, the Orakzais and Turi tribes lived amid the mass of hills and cultivatable valleys. Further south, the Wazir and Mahsud tribes occupied the wooded scrub covered peaks of Waziristan, in the shadow of the Sulaiman Mountain Range. Slicing through this mountainous landscape are four major mountain passes that, according to one authority in the field, "followed the course of the Kabul, Kurram, Tochi and Gomal Rivers. These formed the main arteries of trade and migration, as well as the historic invasion routes into India."[11] Conversely, these mountain passes also offered a path for British imperial aims and ambitions.

Bloody Prelude: The First Afghan War, 1839–1842

The ease with which the British and Indian soldiers of the Army of the Indus toppled the Afghan government, in what would become known as the First Afghan War, was truly astonishing. The objective of the foray into Afghanistan was regime change to replace the existing sovereign with a pro-British ruler. Crossing the Indus River and marching over 1,200 miles across some of the most rugged terrain in the world, the Army of the Indus easily brushed aside Afghan forces determined to contest the invasion. "But subsequent events," wrote Dr. Tony Heathcote; "it would have been recorded as one of the British Indian Army's most successful campaigns."[12] Indeed, the occupation of Kabul in August of 1839 proved a major victory for both the British Army and the English chartered East India Company.

Over the course of the next two years however, the British Army of occupation reduced its numbers, by sending scores of soldiers back to India. At the same time, those officers who remained, sent for their families to join them in Kabul. According to Jules Stewart, the British forces ensconced around the city; "had been lulled into a state of complacency by the ease with which the Afghans had been beaten into submission."[13] While hubris was certainly a factor, inept leadership and major cutbacks in expenditures would also play a key role in the looming catastrophe. When the cost of propping up the new regime (essentially bribing Afghan tribal leaders to support the new ruler) proved too expensive, British authorities reduced disbursements to the eastern Pashtuns (Ghilzais) who were paid not to disrupt the British lines of communications back to India and who also controlled the mountain passes between Kabul and the British fort at Jalalabad, Afghanistan, as well as the strategically important Khyber Pass. At the same time, another British Brigade was sent back to India in an effort to further reduce cost and "Afghanize" the situation.[14]

Displeased by the reduction in their stipend, the Pashtuns immediately shut down the passes between Kabul and Jalalabad. In a portent of what was to come, the tribesmen managed to inflict over 100 casualties on the recently removed British Brigade which was still treading its way east toward Jalalabad. Soon, major tribal uprisings were occurring all around Kabul. In Charikar, north of Kabul, frenzied tribesmen butchered wounded soldiers as well as women and children. By November of 1841, the situation had grown dire for the British garrison outside Kabul. Last minute attempts at negotiations and diplomatic skullduggery proved fruitless. When, in late December, the ranking British political officer was shot and cut into pieces and his remaining body parts staked out at the main gate to the Kabul bazaar by Pashtuns, there remained only one real option for the Kabul garrison. This was to withdraw to the British stronghold in Jalalabad.[15]

A first-rate commander, endeavoring to march the garrison of Kabul 90 miles to Jalalabad in the dead of winter and with thousands of Pashtuns situated in the surrounding mountains and hills, would have found the task almost insurmountable. Unfortunately, the aging and doddering Major General William Elphinstone, commanded the encircled soldiers and civilians. Elphinstone's ineptitude at the battle of Waterloo in 1815 was appreciably exceeded during the winter of 1841 to 1842.[16] As supplies began to dwindle and morale plummeted, "Elphinstone issued and counter-manded orders, demoralizing and confusing his men;" wrote Heathcote. "Finally his commands degenerated into mere suggestions or invitations to use their own judgement."[17]

On the 5th of January in 1842, the garrison began its desperate trek toward Jalalabad. Those too sick or wounded to make the journey were left to the mercy of the Afghans. Traveling through the thin defiles and mountain passes, 4,500 British and Indian soldiers along with a large contingent of British women and children and 12,000 camp followers, staggered east through a canopy of snow and ice. In short order, the Pashtuns commenced nipping at the heels of the rear guard.[18]

On the 13th of January, a lone rider appeared on the frozen plain below the British fortress of Jalalabad. Flinging open the gates of the citadel, a party of British horsemen galloped forward to investigate. To their surprise, they found Dr. William Brydon, an assistant surgeon assigned to the Kabul garrison. He was covered in blood and both horse and rider were barely alive. Brydon was suffering the consequences of a stoning, a gunshot wound to the leg, and several sword cuts to his head and other extremities. As they hurried the wounded man back into the fort, the British soldiers were stunned by his report. With the exception of a small number of hostages held for ransom, the entire column had been slaughtered in the ice-covered corridors between Kabul and Jalalabad. Firing their *jezails* or muskets from the jagged cliffs above and closing in on small groups of British defenders with shield and sword, the tribesmen had destroyed the Kabul garrison.[19]

While many British politicians were now convinced that their forces should withdraw to India, honor demanded revenge for the debacle. "It is impossible to impress upon you too strongly," wrote the celebrated Duke of Wellington to the Governor-General of India, "the Notion of the importance of the restoration of reputation in the east."[20] In February of 1842, a new British commander, Major General George Pollock, arrived in Peshawar in India, determined to restore British prestige. His plan was to march his forces through the Khyber Pass and relieve the garrison at Jalalabad, which had been besieged by the Afghans after the destruction of the Kabul garrison. Pollock then planned to march on Kabul and deal with the hostage situation.[21]

On the 5th of April, Pollock launched his assault on the stoutly defended Khyber Pass. Securing the surrounding peaks in order to protect his flanks and fire down onto the enemy, Pollock stunned the Pashtun defenders by using the tribe's own traditional maneuver. According to Heathcote;

> The surprise was not merely one of timing but of tactics and Pollock entered Pathan folklore as the first plains-dwelling general to use the Pathan technique of seizing the high ground or 'crowning the heights.' Flanking columns clambered up the hills on either side of the road, each party with its buglers warned to sound the 'advance' or 'halt' if they got too far ahead or behind its neighbours. Now it was the turn of the Pathans to be shot down by fire from above.[22]

By the end of the day, the British had seized the Khyber Pass and routed the defenders. While the tactics employed by Pollock against the Pashtuns were simple and consistent with age-old military principles, it would be one of many lessons surprisingly difficult for the British to retain over the course of the next hundred years.[23]

By September, Pollock recaptured Kabul and secured the release of the hostages. In October however, the British once again abandoned the capital and withdrew their forces back to India. They would not make the same mistake twice. Seizing control of Kabul had proven simple. Occupying the country and maintaining lines of communications with India through Pashtun tribal areas on the other hand, was judged to be unworkable. As historian Alan Warren pointed out, the British "correctly concluded that the task of governing Afghanistan was beyond the scope of India's resources."[24] Nevertheless, for the British it would not be their last war with Afghanistan and it would certainly not be the last time they confronted the Pashtun tribes of the North-West Frontier.

Notes

1. Barbara D. Metcalf and Thomas R. Metcalf, *A Concise History of Modern India* (Second edition) (Cambridge, UK: Cambridge University Press, 2006), 68, 90.

2. Thomas H. Johnson and M. Chris Mason, "No Sign Until the Burst of Fire: Understanding the Pakistan-Afghanistan Frontier," *International Security*, Vol. 32, No. 4 (Spring 2008), 51.

3. David Dichter, *The North-West Frontier of West Pakistan: A Study in Regional Geography* (Oxford, UK: Clarendon Press, 1967), 3.

4. Charles Allen, *God's Terrorists: The Wahhabi Cult and the Hidden Roots of Modern Jihad* (Cambridge, MA: Da Capo Press, 2006), 2.

5. Sher Muhammad Mohmand, *The Pathan Customs* (Peshawar, Pakistan: n.p., 2003), 1–2.

6. Mohmand, 42.

7. Ganesh Sitaraman, "The Land of 10,000 Wars," *The New York Times*, 17 August 2009.

8. Ganesh Sitaraman, "The Land of 10,000 Wars," *The New York Times*, 17 August 2009.

9. Mohmand, 1–2, 42.

10. Dichter, 7–8; T. R. Moreman, *The Army of India and the Development of Frontier Warfare* (London: Macmillan Press Ltd., 1998), 1.

11. T.R. Moreman, 1–2.

12. T.A. Heathcote, *The Afghan Wars 1839–1919* (Kent, UK: Spellmount, 2003), 42–43.

13. Jules Stewart, *The Khyber Rifles: From the British Raj to Al Qaeda* (Phoenix Mill, UK: Sutton Publishing Ltd., 2005), 3.

14. Heathcote, 52; Stewart, 4; Michael Barthorp, *Afghan Wars and the North-West Frontier 1839–1947* (London: Cassell, 1982), 37.

15. Barthorp, 37; Heathcote, 53, 57; Stewart, 4; John H. Waller, *Beyond The Khyber Pass: The Road to British Disaster in the First Afghan War* (New York, NY: Random House, 1990), 232–235; Charles Miller, *Khyber: British India's North-West Frontier: The Story of an Imperial Migraine* (New York: Macmillan, 1977), 65–68.

16. Alessandro Barbero, *The Battle: A New History of Waterloo*, trans. John Cullen (New York: Walker & Company, 2003), 266–267.

17. Heathcote, 58.

18. Heathcote, 58.

19. Barthorp, 3; Waller, 254–255; Miller, 79; Heathcote, 63.

20. Heathcote, 72.

21. Heathcote, 68.

22. Heathcote, 68–69.

23. Miller, 83.

24. Alan Warren, *Waziristan, the Faqir of Ipi and the Indian Army: The North-West Frontier Revolt of 1936–1937* (Oxford, UK: Oxford University Press, 2000), xx.

Chapter 2

"Discomfiture Might Suffice As Punishment"
British Military Operations on the North-West Frontier
1849–1900

The general attitude of the tribes is at present neither peaceful nor submissive.

General Report on the Administration of the Punjab,
1849–1851

There are many pensioned or discharged officers and soldiers among them who doubtless impart the military training they themselves acquired in the ranks of the Native Army.

British General Sir William Lockhart

The Punjab Irregular Force

With the successful conclusion of the Second Sikh War in 1849, the British East India Company officially annexed the Punjab. The Company was now neighbors with the population living west of the Indus River and the long running troubles between the Sikhs and the Pashtun tribes of the North-West Frontier became a British problem. The new custodians of Punjab faced the daunting task of protecting the border areas from trans-border Pashtun raids and assaults. This is something the Sikhs had never been able to prevent.[1]

The new British administration in Punjab attempted to introduce a conciliatory policy toward the tribes. There would be no encroachment by the British past the foothills of Punjab. This guiding principle was, to a degree, rooted in the terrible recollections of the First Afghan War. According to the British historian T.R. Moreman "Tribal independence was recognized and they were actively encouraged to trade with British India, given access to medical and other assistance, and allowed to enlist in the ranks of the police and military forces to promote friendly relations. British officials were also expressly forbidden to go into tribal territory to minimize incidents in what was commonly known as the 'close border' policy."[2] Over 100,000 well-armed Pashtun tribesmen confronted the British, determined to continue their highly profitable raids into Punjab. That the East India Company was exceedingly worried about the tribes is confirmed in early testimony by its directors:

The sense which our predecessors entertained of their prowess," the report noted; "is attested by the forts now standing and by the tumuli, at short intervals all down the Derajat, on which military posts were probably placed 1,500 years ago to oppose them. They are not capable of combination but they could make desultory attacks in ceaseless succession. It is clear that, if unopposed, they would devastate the . . . country down to the Indus and threaten our Cis-Indus districts. Thus, to guard the line of the Indus, a greater force would be required than that now employed.[3]

This new military contingent was designated as the Punjab Irregular Force (PIF). The organization was composed initially of five infantry regiments and five cavalry regiments, as well as three light or mountain batteries which were designed along the same lines as the irregular forces employed by the British Bengal Army in India. An elite force formed primarily of Pashtuns called the "Queen's Own Corps of Guides", was also created. Fashioned to guide regular army units and perform scouting missions, the Guides would become legendary on the North-West Frontier. Four British officers, 16 native officers and 96 non-commissioned officers were assigned to each regiment with its ranks composed of Sikhs, Pashtuns, Gurkhas, Punjabi Muslims, and others.[4]

A few of the British officers assigned to the PIF had served in the First Afghan War and were somewhat familiar with the trans-border Pashtun tribes. For the cost of three rupees, British officers unacquainted with commanding and training irregular forces could turn to Captain Charles Farquhar Trower's *Hints on Irregular Cavalry: Its Conformation, Management and Use in Both A Military and Political Point of View*. Published in Calcutta in 1845, Trower's work was an unofficial publication designed to aid British officers unfamiliar with irregular forces. Having commanded a myriad of native irregulars in India, Trower's notes on the training and oversight of local forces is as important today as it was in the mid-nineteenth century, particularly his assessments of how to work with the Pashtun tribes.[5]

"It is," wrote Trower, "universally admitted, that the efficiency of native soldiers generally depends on their European Officers."[6] An officer, he pointed out, should,

> be able to converse really fluently with those entrusted to him. He should be well versed in their customs, habits, and peculiar modes of thinking and feeling, which can alone be acquired by mixing much with natives. He should be a man of admirable temper, never hasty, firm and yet pa-

tient. For many things apparently trifling to our ideas, are of much importance in their estimation and it is a great, although a frequent, mistake to judge of the conduct of natives by the standard which we have set up for our own.[7]

Trower also maintained that; "mixing with the men in their warlike sports creates affection, as the excelling [of] them in their own line produces admiration."[8]

Trower was convinced that the Pashtun tribesmen made the finest irregular cavalry. "They are generally illiterate, haughty and turbulent," he wrote, "but they are gallant and true, hard-working and zealous, and even with a little kindness and tact in their management, make such troops as no one need hesitate to lead where the blows are most rife."[9] The captain also pointed out that there was "a strong feeling of clanship" between the Pashtuns and "they are peculiarly sensitive to the opinion of their own '*Khel*' or '*Zye*.'" In the end, Trower understood it was the treatment the Pashtun received "which will make them either cheerful and zealous soldiers or useless rabble." He continued:

There is none however, who can less bear rudeness or offensive language and he must never be submitted to either. He must feel that he is certain of being well received by his officer. Nothing in treatment or obedience should be imposed on, or required of the soldier which may tend to lower him in his own estimation or in that of his fellows in or out of service. An officer who has not had much intimacy with natives of this description, even with the best intentions, may unwillingly offend and annoy them from his very ignorance.[10]

Trower was also convinced that officers should; "Have nothing to say to their [Pashtuns'] private and domestic affairs. You will thus escape much trouble and considerable ill-will."[11]

The PIF was placed under the control of the Board of Administration of the Punjab, removing it from regular army control. In his book *The Army in India and the Development of Frontier Warfare, 1849-1947*, T.R. Moreman contended that; "This decision to localize the PIF solely for duty in the Punjab gave the Board of Administration almost complete control of the troops stationed along the border, enabling it to quickly respond to raids or other developments without constant recourse to the central government for military support."[12] British political officers were also appointed to work with the military and "held sway" over the armed forces.[13]

In what would become known as a "watch and ward" mission, the PIF positioned units in every district, establishing quick reaction forces to prohibit raids into the border region and to chase down Pashtun brigands before they could escape to the safety of their mountain refuge. A road running parallel to the border was quickly built as were a series of outposts and forts. "Cavalry regiments;" wrote Moreman, "along with small detachments of infantry, were dispersed in a chain of small mud forts, blockhouses, and outposts that blocked valleys, ravines, and other lines of approach leading down from the hills used by raiding gangs. The intervening ground between these posts was systematically patrolled by cavalry detachments to deter raids, gather intelligence, and attempt to intercept parties of marauders following attacks on local villages."[14]

In spite of these arrangements, the 700 mile border proved virtually impossible to defend against tribal raids. Pashtun raiders continued to infiltrate from the frontier into Punjab. Despite the support of a large contingent of regular troops from the Bengal Army of India that had been sent to the Peshawar District to guard against Afghan incursions, Pashtun marauders continued to commit depredations all along the border. The East India Company's Court of Directors was so astonished by their prowess that they described the Pashtun intruders in near herculean prose in an early report to the government. They wrote; "The mountaineers can both attack and fly with the utmost rapidity, all of them being active footmen and many of them being mounted on small and hardy cattle, capable not only of making extraordinary marches in the open country and threading the rough narrow glens and passes of the hills but also of ascending their sides and literally passing over rocks, hillocks, and ridges that a mere denizen of the plains would not dare to face."[15]

The construction of 15 forts and 50 outposts and the stationing of 12,800 irregular and 10,821 regular soldiers in Punjab by 1855, did little to quell the forays. While British political officers tried their best to maintain amity with the tribes of the North-West Frontier, the constant raiding by the Pashtuns forced them to retaliate against the tribes. Frequently, these retaliatory measures included curtailing payments to the clans, hostage taking, fines, trading blockades, and the withdrawal of economic development. Many times these corrective measures proved successful;. When they did not however, the British often resorted to punitive expeditions that were soon given the implacable moniker of "butcher and bolt."[16]

These punitive expeditions were also called "harry and hurry" and "tip and run." They were often the last resort for British officials attempting to bring an errant tribe back into line. On more than one occasion, Pashtuns refused to turn over wanted criminals to the British authorities as this violated the Pashtun code of *Pashtunwali*. This refusal triggered a punitive expedition. Significantly, this is the same code which today allows the Taliban and al-Qaida to find sanctuary with the trans-border Pashtun tribes. The code is also a societal paradigm that the US Army and other western forces have struggled to comprehend in the years since 2001.[17]

The "butcher and bolt" operations often included the destruction of Pashtun villages, crops, concealed provisions, and supplies of water. According to one historian, the expeditions were designed to create the maximum inconvenience and total bankruptcy.[18] While not every British commander and soldier favored these techniques, many believed it was the best solution to the problem short of occupying the entire North-West Frontier, a remedy that at the time, was completely unacceptable to the government. British commander Sir Richard Temple concluded in 1855:

> When an expedition is undertaken, then if the enemy were to assemble in force and take up a position and offer battle, they could be attacked and defeated and their discomfiture might suffice as punishment, without any further measure. In that event, the affair would be conducted after the manner of regular warfare.[19]

Temple quickly identified operations in the frontier region as something other than regular warfare:

> In civilized warfare, force is directed against the armed enemy and his defensible positions but not against his country and subjects, who may be morally unconcerned in the hostilities and innocent of offence. However, *this is not civilized warfare.* The enemy does not possess troops that stand to be attacked nor defensible posts to be taken nor innocent subjects to be spared. He has only rough hills to be penetrated, robber fastnesses to be scaled, and dwellings containing people, all of them to a man concerned in hostilities.[20]

In summing up the key to achieving victory over the rebellious Pashtuns, Temple made it clear that the Pashtun population could be considered combatants. He claimed; "To spare these villages would be about as reasonable as to spare the commissariat supplies or arsenals of a civilized enemy."[21]

Carrying out these operations in Pashtun territory was no easy task. An expedition would have to be supported by a lengthy logistical column forced to snake its way through the narrow valley floors and across dry riverbeds and other precipitous and challenging terrain. More often than not, wheeled transport could not maneuver through this type of terrain, forcing the expedition to rely on pack mules. "As there was a limit to the number of men and pack animals that could move over one road in daylight;" wrote Moreman, "large forces normally had to be broken into several columns and moved by separate routes."[22] These columns were of course, extremely vulnerable to attack from a Pashtun *lashkar* perched in the mountains above the slow moving force. As Moreman has pointed out; "*Lashkars* excelled at desultory hit-and-run guerrilla warfare, attacking isolated parties of troops, raiding convoys on the lines of communication, sniping foraging parties, and attacking rear guards at the end of each day's operation."[23] While many of the tribesmen within a *lashkar* were armed with swords, knives, and shields, countless others were able to acquire the *jezail* which was a locally manufactured muzzle-loading musket. In both range and accuracy however, the *jezail* surpassed the Brown Bess muskets employed by the British during the early years on the North-West Frontier.

Fifteen major "butcher and bolt" expeditions were conducted between 1849 and 1857.[24] T.R. Moreman has noted that; "By trial and error, the PIF evolved a series of specialized principles and minor tactics tailored to local conditions in tribal territory. To meet tribesmen on equal terms, its infantry regiments developed light infantry skills, skirmishing skills, skill at arms, marksmanship skills, self-reliance skills, and fieldcraft. These [skills] were modeled on those of their opponents. Mountain artillery batteries were equipped with light ordnance [which was] capable of being dismantled and transported in the hills on muleback."[25]

The main objective of British and Indian soldiers was to bring about a large engagement with the Pashtun tribes in order to inflict as many casualties as possible and thus discourage the enemy and bring him to terms. Many times however, this type of punitive action proved unsuccessful. Whereupon, the British Army in India often resorted to burning villages and crops in order to chastise and dishearten the tribesmen. As Pollock had done years before in his operation in the Khyber Pass, British and Indian soldiers moving against tribes protected themselves by maintaining the high ground. *Piquets*, which is a French term for outpost or guard, were almost always positioned on the high ground to protect the slow moving columns as they inched their way into tribal territory. As the columns passed the *piquets* would pack up and either move to a new location or join the column. It was indeed a dangerous undertaking as the tribes were frequently waiting to assail the outpost while it was being built or during its withdrawal.[26]

Night encampments also had to be protected. These military camps were ringed by *piquets* with the main force ensconced behind sturdy barricades made of rocks, ammo boxes, or whatever material could be found to protect against tribal snipers and massed attacks by sword-wielding Pashtuns. While marching into tribal territory to conduct a "butcher and bolt" mission was always risky, the withdrawal phase of the operation often proved the most dangerous. More often than not, the Pashtuns would attack the rear guard elements during this delicate phase of the expedition. "The brutal treatment frequently meted out to British or Indian dead and wounded by tribesmen;" wrote Moreman, "exerted a powerful influence on hill warfare which necessitated rapid counterattacks to recover the dead bodies and prisoners, as they could not be allowed to fall into enemy hands."[27]

An operation carried out in 1850 provides insight to how many of these actions were conducted. While the British disbursed a large annual subsidy to an Afridis' *khel* to maintain security in the Kohat Pass, 1,000 of their tribesmen attacked a small group of British engineers constructing a road, killing and wounding many. Soon, an expeditionary force was marching toward the Kohat Pass. As the column advanced, a Punjab infantry regiment picketed the surrounding peaks. As the British approached the village of Akhor, the *maliks* (tribal elders) came forward to meet them and state their case. The British commanders told the *maliks* that they had one hour to surrender and turn over all their weapons. After briefly discussing the matter, the elders refused these British terms. Immediately, elements of the PIF crowned the heights around the village while horse artillery and infantry formed for an assault. [28] Stationed behind a stone breastwork or *sangar*, the tribesmen put up a gallant but brief defense. Once the village was captured, it was partly destroyed.

Marching into the pass, the British sent pickets to the high ground and encamped for the night. Thus far, the operation had gone off without a hitch. However, this was only because the Pashtuns had been unable to exploit a British mistake. In the morning, as the pickets manning the heights around the pass were relieved, the Pashtuns found their chance to strike. An Indian officer failed to follow the correct procedures in relieving the pickets, neglecting to provide security as they were coming off the mountain. From their hiding places, the Afridis quickly assailed the pickets and wounded several. The attackers were eventually driven back by the horse artillery.

Before marching out of the pass, corrective measures were applied by the British command to ensure that everyone understood proper picket procedures and, as a result, the return march home proved uneventful. One historian of the North-West Frontier wrote that; "As expedition followed expedition and the tribesmen grew more and more expert at 'reading' the movements of troops, the relief of pickets and the relative positions of advance and rear guards as well as the main bodies of columns, had to be regulated with absolute precision if trouble were to be avoided. The whole business in fact, became a battle drill."[29] Like the Taliban of today, the Pashtuns of the mid-nineteenth century were exceedingly capable of shifting tactics and exploiting mistakes. History would show that if their enemies were not fully versed and practiced in this type of warfare, that the outcome often led to disastrous consequences.

Between 1849 and 1886, the PIF (whose name was changed to the Punjab Frontier Force or PFF, in 1865) acquired valuable skills in fighting the Pashtuns in the rugged mountainous terrain of the North-West Frontier. It was soon realized that these operations were poles apart from operations conducted elsewhere and required new tactics and skill sets. Native contingents within the PIF who were familiar with this type of warfare, proved invaluable in helping to implement many of these procedures. In 1862, a new Frontier Militia was created. Its members were Pashtun tribesmen and, according to one source, they provided local knowledge, acted as guides, and collected valuable intelligence regarding raids and offences committed by the trans-border tribes.[30] The new militia also provided employment to Pashtuns, who might otherwise have been involved in continued criminal activity. The Pashtun militiamen proved immensely successful and greatly increased the effectiveness of the PIF.

Throughout this period, many British officers were troubled by the Regular Army's lack of training in frontier warfare. Regular Army soldiers of the Bengal Army who were posted to Peshawar, rarely conducted punitive expeditions and trained almost exclusively in conventional tactics. They also lacked the light logistical transport needed to conduct campaigns in the tribal regions of the North-West Frontier. The Irregular Forces on the other hand, trained constantly in mountain warfare as well as in light infantry tactics which emphasized individual initiative and continually sharpened their skills by participating in numerous expeditions.

A British Commissioner assigned to Peshawar in this period noted that frontier warfare required special training. The simple transfer of regular forces to the area, he believed, would always fail. The commissioner explained:

I have no hesitation in saying that troops freshly and indiscriminately brought to the work must fail even physically, they would break down. I can assure the government that I have seen sepoys of the Regular Army shot down and cut down on the hillside, perfectly helpless, whilst their comrades of the Irregular Force have been driving the enemy up a neighbouring hill and if you look to smaller matters (which in truth make up the efficiency of the whole) we shall see how the Irregular of the Punjab Force excels [over] his comrade in the Regular Army.[31]

Moreover, according to the commissioner, the nature of operations dictated a dispersed disposition of forces, making the competency and initiative of the lower level leaders of critical importance. He asserted; "It is necessary to occupy many points and to keep up communications with them all. This involves the detachment of many parties, and Native Officers and Non-Commissioned Officers are frequently commanding small but important posts which requires intelligence, care, and prudence of mind [as well as] knowledge of the enemy's tactics."[32]

As an illustration, during the disastrous Second Afghan War (1878–1880), the regular British-Indian Army struggled to conduct irregular mountain warfare against the Pashtun tribes, while the PFF performed remarkably well. Since the PFF fell under the purview of the Punjab Government instead of the British military command, little attempt had been made to disseminate irregular doctrine and tactics to the regular forces. As T.R. Moreman has pointed out, the PFF was not responsible for the circulation of tactical information beyond the few regulars that had fought alongside it on active service. As long as PFF units could cope with fighting tribesmen with limited outside assistance, there was simply no need to develop a tactical doctrine for training the rest of the British and Indian armies.[33] In 1886, the PFF was finally placed under the control of the British military. However, it would take a massive Pashtun uprising to convince the British of the need to publish new training manuals and to train the entire regular force in frontier warfare.

The Pashtun Revolt of 1897-1898

In July 1897, Wazir tribesmen murdered a British political officer in Northern Waziristan while he participated in a *jirga* (council). A Pashtun mullah, known by some as the "Mullah of Swat," had generated the unrest. The British more commonly referred to this firebrand as the "Mad Mullah." Following the assassination, the British moved swiftly to punish the culprits, advancing two brigades into Waziristan. The force consisted of veteran units well versed in frontier warfare. The brigades, designated as the Tochi Field Force, quickly quelled the rebellion and punished the wayward tribesmen.[34]

Unfortunately for the British, the rebellion soon spread outside of Northern Waziristan, fanned by the Mad Mullah's call for a *jihad* against the infidels. On the 26th of July, a sizeable *lashkar* laid siege to a British fort at Chakdara near the Malakand Pass. Heavy attacks by sword and knife carrying Pashtuns led to bloody close quarters combat and nearly succeeded in overrunning the entire command. Enemy fighters in fact managed to enter a portion of the camp held by the engineers and remove a large quantity of ammunition before being forced back. Tribesmen armed with modern rifles also shot down scores of British and Indian soldiers. By the first week of August, British reinforcements, the Malakand Field Force, arrived and the siege was lifted. During the ensuing weeks, the British once again directed punitive operations against the tribesmen, this time in the Swat Valley.[35]

The retaliation had little effect on the tribes and the rebellion again spread. Pashtun tribes, aided by their Afghan brethren, launched an assault on a British fort in the Peshawar District on the 7th of August. By September, the new Mohmand Field Force joined the Malakand Field Force and set out to punish the tribes responsible for the attack in the Peshawar District. Both the Mohmand Field Force and the Malakand Field Force were seriously mauled in the ensuing actions. Large numbers of Pashtun tribesmen armed with Martini-Henrys and Remington rifles, used long-range fire to cut down advancing British and Indian soldiers, attacking with swords and knives only when their enemy conducted a withdrawal or committed a serious tactical error. The operation resulted in many missteps, leading to hundreds of British and Indian casualties. Although the British were finally able to bring the responsible tribes to terms, the brief campaign was marked by a lack of frontier skills on the part of many British and Indian soldiers and by the tactical expertise of the Pashtuns. "There is no doubt that our officers and men have much to learn in regard to keeping together and seeing to mutual support and to the ground, when they get away from direct authority;" wrote the commander of the expedition. "All the mishaps that have occurred here are traceable to carelessness on these points, which is brought out by the superior smartness of the enemy."[36]

While the British had come to terms with the tribesmen who had attacked the Peshawar District, the conflict was not yet at an end. In the Khyber Pass region, the rebellion continued as the Afridis and Orakzais tribes formed *lashkars* and launched attacks against local levies.

Map 3. The Pashtun Revolt of 1897-1898.

The famed unit known as the Khyber Rifles was soon forced to surrender along with a sizable amount of their Snider rifles and ammunition.[37] To put down the rebellion, the British formed an enormous new force christened as The Tirah Expeditionary Force. This new command contained over

34,000 combat soldiers as well as over 19,000 combat support personnel supported by 34,000 pack animals. This sizable force faced nearly 50,000 tribesmen, many of who were heavily armed with modern rifles. Many of the tribesmen were also veterans from the Indian Army and as Moreman has remarked; "[They were] aware of the tactics employed by imperial troops."[38]

In the campaign that followed, the tribesmen used their modern rifles with deadly effect. British and Indian soldiers from the regular army, accustomed to slow and measured volley fire and untrained in frontier warfare, were no match for the tribesmen who used cover and concealment to fire down on the slow moving columns. In one engagement, a British and Indian battalion suffered 172 casualties while assaulting Pashtuns armed with quick-firing rifles. In many cases British artillery proved ineffective as clever tribesmen sought shelter in mountain fissures and other advantageous defensive positions. The Afridis and Orakzais soundly out shot and out maneuvered the slow and tactically inefficient expeditionary force. "The Afridis and Orakzais appear to be as well armed as our native troops;" wrote a high-ranking British officer. "There are many pensioned or discharged officers and soldiers among them who doubtless impart the military training they have themselves acquired in the ranks of the Native Army."[39] These men not only conveyed their knowledge of British tactical methods to their fellow tribesmen but developed new tactics based on their familiarity with the British system. As the British would find out more than once, the ally one trains and arms can suddenly become the enemy one has prepared and equipped.

It would take until April of 1898 to bring the tribes to terms. By that date, British and Indian forces had suffered almost 2,000 casualties from the frontier rebellion. In the Tirah Campaign alone, the expeditionary force had suffered over 1,000 casualties. An unidentified British officer wrote during the campaign; "Tirah is but the history of a failure, redeemed by gallant pluck and endurance of the fighting ranks and their officers."[40] He was probably not far off the mark in his observations. By the end of the campaign, the British Army in India began to issue new handbooks to its soldiers and institute a new training regime that was specifically designed to improve its capabilities in frontier warfare. While great improvements were made, the true test of these new methods could only be measured by renewed operations against the Pashtuns.

Notes

1. Michael Barthorp, *Afghan Wars and the North-West Frontier 1839–1947* (London: Cassell, 1982), 49; T.R. Moreman, "'The Greatest Training Ground in the World:' The Army in India and the North-West Frontier 1901–1947," in *A Military History of India and South Asia from the East India Company to the Nuclear Era* edited by Daniel P. Marston and Chandar S. Sundaram (Westport, CT: Praeger Security International, 2007), 53–54; T.A. Heathcote, *The Indian Army: The Garrison of British Imperial India, 1822–1922* (New York, NY: Hippocrene Books, 1974), 27.

2. T.R. Moreman, *The Army in India and the Development of Frontier Warfare, 1849–1947*, (London: Macmillan Press Ltd., 1998), 5

3. *General Report on the Administration of the Punjab for the Years 1849–50 and 1850–1851* (London: Printed for the Court of Directors of the East India Company, 1854), 18.

4. T.R. Moreman, *The Army in India and the Development of Frontier Warfare, 1849–1947*, 6; Barthorp, *Afghan Wars and the North-West Frontier 1839–1947*, 51; Charles Miller, *Khyber: British India's North-West Frontier: The Story of an Imperial Migraine* (New York: Macmillan, 1977), 113; Rajit K. Mazumder, *The Indian Army and the Making of Punjab* (Delhi, India: Permanent Black, 2003), 8.

5. T.R. Moreman, *The Army in India and the Development of Frontier Warfare, 1849–1947*, 6; Captain Charles Farquhar Trower, *Hints on Irregular Cavalry, Its Conformation, Management and Use in Both a Military and Political Point of View* (Calcutta, India: W. Thacker and Co., 1845).

6. Trower, 6.

7. Trower, 7–8.

8. Trower, 7–8.

9. Trower, 41.

10. Trower, 42.

11. Trower, 47

12. T.R. Moreman, *The Army in India and the Development of Frontier Warfare, 1849–1947*, 6.

13. Arthur Swinson, *North-West Frontier: People and Events, 1839–1947* (New York: Praeger, 1967), 102–103.

14. T.R. Moreman, *The Army in India and the Development of Frontier Warfare, 1849–1947*, 6–7.

15. *General Report on the Administration of the Punjab for the Years 1849–1850 and 1850–1851*, 31.

16. T.R. Moreman, *The Army in India and the Development of Frontier Warfare, 1849–1947*, 8; Charles Chenevix Trench, *The Frontier Scouts* (London, UK: Jonathan Cape, 1985), 2.

17. T.R. Moreman, *The Army in India and the Development of Frontier Warfare, 1849–1947*, 8–9; Miller, 116; Thomas H. Johnson and M. Chris Mason, "No Sign Until the Burst of Fire: Understanding the Pakistan-Afghanistan Frontier," *International Security*, Vol. 32, No. 4 (Spring 2008), 64.

18. T.R. Moreman, *The Army in India and the Development of Frontier Warfare, 1849–1947*, 8–9; Miller, 116.

19. T.R. Moreman, *The Army in India and the Development of Frontier Warfare, 1849–1947*, 6.

20. T.R. Moreman, *The Army in India and the Development of Frontier Warfare, 1849–1947*, 6.21.

22. T.R. Moreman, *The Army in India and the Development of Frontier Warfare, 1849–1947*, 9.

23. T.R. Moreman, *The Army in India and the Development of Frontier Warfare, 1849–1947*, 6.

24. Barthorp, 52.

25. T.R. Moreman, "'Passing It On:'" The Army in India and Frontier Warfare, 1914–39" in *War and Society in Colonial India 1807–1945* edited by Kaushik Roy (Oxford, UK: Oxford University Press, 2006), 276–277.

26. T.R. Moreman, "'Passing It On:'" The Army in India and Frontier Warfare, 1914–39," 276–277.

27. T.R. Moreman, "'Passing It On:'" The Army in India and Frontier Warfare, 1914–39," 277.

28. Swinson, 105–106.

29. Swinson, 106.

30. T.R. Moreman, *The Army in India and the Development of Frontier Warfare, 1849–1947*, 23.

31. Quoted in T.R. Moreman, *The Army in India and the Development of Frontier Warfare, 1849–1947*, 22.

32. Quoted in T.R. Moreman, *The Army in India and the Development of Frontier Warfare, 1849–1947*, 22.

33. T.R. Moreman, *The Army in India and the Development of Frontier Warfare, 1849–1947*, 35.

34. T.R. Moreman, *The Army in India and the Development of Frontier Warfare, 1849–1947*, 53–54; Swinson, 232–233.

35. Swinson, 232; Captain H.L. Nevill, *Campaigns on the North-West Frontier* (Nashville, TN: The Battery Press, 1912), 226; T.R. Moreman, *The Army in India and the Development of Frontier Warfare, 1849–1947*, 54.

36. T.R. Moreman, *The Army in India and the Development of Frontier Warfare, 1849–1947*, 54–55.

37. For a complete history of this engagement, see Jules Stewart, *The Khyber Rifles: From the British Raj to Al Qaeda* (Phoenix Mill, UK: Sutton Publishing Ltd., 2005), 121–156.

38. T.R. Moreman, *The Army in India and the Development of Frontier Warfare, 1849–1947*, 57.

39. Quoted in T.R. Moreman, *The Army in India and the Development of Frontier Warfare, 1849–1947*, 62–63.

40. Quoted in T.R. Moreman, *The Army in India and the Development of Frontier Warfare, 1849–1947*, 68, 71.

Chapter 3

"I Doubt If It Is Understood How Desperate the Fighting Has Been During This Operation"
British Military Operations on the North-West Frontier
1900–1920

> A military operation in Waziristan always seemed to exceed its predecessor in carnage.
>
> Charles Miller

> For many years . . . we followed the policy of non-interference with the inhabitants . . . We hoped that if we left them alone, they would leave us alone.
>
> Lord Chelmsford, Viceroy of India, August 1920

The 1908 Zakka *Khel* and Mohmand Expeditions

In the aftermath of the Tirah campaign, the British Army in India introduced new frontier warfare training manuals and established a new training regime for its regular forces. In addition, the de-localization of the PFF in 1903 significantly cut down on the problems associated with sustaining a sole specialized force in Punjab. In February of 1908, after a series of raids by the Zakka *Khel* Afridis, the new training program was put to the test.[1]

Major General Sir James Willcocks' Bazar Valley Expeditionary Force mobilized and marched quickly out of Peshawar, a bare minimum of logistical transports bolstering the speed of the columns. While Willcocks marched his main force directly on the Zakka *Khel* stronghold, the 800 men of the Khyber Rifles, whose ranks included a number of Afridis from the Zakka *Khel*, moved swiftly around the errant tribesmen and sealed off any possible escape route into Afghanistan. Forty-eight hours into the operation, the Khyber Rifles blocked all passes into the Bazar Valley as Willcocks' main force proceeded to thrash the tribesmen with their new ten-pounder guns and direct assaults. Within a week, the Zekka *Khel* was completely crushed. Incapable of further resistance, the tribesmen sued for peace on the 28th of February.[2]

The campaign proved so successful that the press christened it the "weekend war." The Zakka *Khel* suffered staggering losses while the British and Indian forces lost three soldiers. According to one source; "The Zakka *Khel* had suffered casualties far in excess of those lost in the Tirah

Expedition with every family in the Bazar Valley suffering losses from amongst its fighting men."[3] The commander of the Khyber Rifles reported that; "The Afridis, who are no mean judges of hill fighting, express themselves amazed at the handling and conduct of the troops as unlike anything they have seen or heard of and the fact that they have obtained no loot in mules, rifles, stores, or ammunition on which they confidently counted to compensate for their own losses, has given them a strong distaste for expeditions conducted on these novel lines."[4]

A few months later, Willcocks launched a comparable operation against the Mohmands with almost identical results. Beyond a doubt, the new frontier warfare training manuals and new training methods implemented by the British and Indian regulars after the 1897–1898 campaigns, were proving highly successful. As one senior British official pointed out:

> From a military point of view the most satisfactory features of the expedition were the ease and rapidity with which it was sent off without any dislocation of the separate commands, the excellence of the transport and supply arrangements, the signaling communications, and above all the unexampled efficiency of the troops themselves in their knowledge of hill fighting. They proved as good or even better than the Zakkas themselves among their own hills. It speaks volumes for the pains bestowed on their training.

The official saw the training as the key to a military turning point in the campaign against the Zakka enemy, noting that; "In 1897 the superiority of the tribes over us in the hills was very marked and we suffered heavily, whilst I believe the Zakka loss on the present occasion exceeds the whole tribal loss in the Tirah campaign and our own loss has been extremely small."[5]

Unfortunately, British accomplishments in hill warfare would be short lived. In 1909, the British General Staff in India did away with the handbooks and instruction manuals produced after the frontier uprisings of 1897–1898. Citing a need for more standardized training, the General Staff introduced *Field Service Regulations* that were to be implemented by all British and Indian forces. "Thenceforth," wrote military historian T.R. Moreman; "British and Indian troops relied for guidance in frontier fighting on the general principles of war and six condensed paragraphs that only provided a bare outline of the specialized tactics required in tribal territory."[6] At first, the new regulations had little effect as many British and Indian soldiers were well versed in frontier fighting and could rely on their past experience in conducting operations against the tribes. The eruption of the First World War in 1914, however, would completely change the state of affairs on the North-West Frontier and a new wave of violence would find British and Indian forces sadly lacking in the expertise needed to conduct hill warfare against the Pashtun tribes.

As the First World War intensified and casualties increased, veteran frontier fighting units from the British Indian Army were assigned to various fronts around the world. Although their replacements were well equipped, they possessed little experience in tribal warfare. These units of the British Territorial Army (TA) not only lacked training in hill warfare but were also deficient in basic combat skills and training. Regrettably, they had only the *Field Service Manual* to turn to as manuals for conducting frontier warfare had been removed from the system in 1909. As one historian pointed out; "The inherent limitations of relying solely on the principles of war and limited information contained in the FSR [*Field Service Manual*] to govern frontier warfare training were exposed."[7] Outbreaks of tribal violence from 1915–1918 confirmed the vulnerability of the TA and, even though a Mountain Warfare School was set up in 1916 to assist newcomers, the new training program had little effect on the replacements.

A senior British officer in 1917 went so far as to say that he thought frontier warfare was a science:

> I have always regarded it as a thing very much like chess which wants a great deal of skill to avoid mistakes but at the same time it is not a science that can be said at any one time to have reached its finality. We are always going on evolving new things and a great many of these points that have been raised have been evolved gradually from experience. We must not assume that the stage we have reached now is the last stage in the process. We must remember that the increased armament of these tribes that we fight against will go on modifying our rules and systems.[8]

Indeed, by 1917, the tribes of the North-West Frontier had increased their armaments substantially, equipping themselves on a massive scale with new breech-loading magazine-fed rifles, all of which used smokeless powder. For example, a British historian noted that; "Tribal made versions of the Martini-Henri and Lee-Enfield rifles had became the principal Mahsud weapon."[9] The lack of trained, skilled, frontier fighters combined with the improved weaponry of the tribes would lead to what General Sir Charles Monro, the British Commander-in-Chief in India would later call; "unparalleled hard fighting and severity."[10]

The Third Afghan War and the Campaign in Waziristan 1919–1920

On the 4th of May in 1919, the military forces of Afghanistan, in an effort to regain control of external relations from the British, crossed the Durand Line into the North-West Frontier and set off what one high ranking statesman called "the most meaningless, crazy and unnecessary war in history."[11] It was clear from the beginning that the Afghans intended to use the tribes of the North-West Frontier to assist in their operations against British forces. Calling for a *jihad* and inciting the Pashtun tribes with the promise of money and weapons, the Afghan regular army quickly seized Bagh near the strategically important Khyber Pass. A large Afghan force also occupied Dakka, about ten miles west of Bagh. Twenty-five miles to the east in Peshawar, the British Army began preparations to eject the invaders.[12]

The British and Indian forces had little trouble defeating the Afghan regulars and quickly recaptured Bagh and Dakka. At Dakka, the British were also able to effectively divide the Mohmands and Afridis and thwart their plans to combine forces with the Afghan regular army. Afghan offensives into Chitral and Baluchistan were also swiftly repulsed by British and Indian forces. Strangely enough, the defeat of the Afghan regular army in the Khyber region only served to bolster the hostility of the Pashtun tribes. As one historian pointed out; "The successive Afghan defeats at Bagh and Dakka could have been expected to damp down any thoughts that the Mohmands and Afridi tribes on either side if the Khyber might have had of coming out in support of their co-religionist but old habits die hard and with what might seem curious timing, the British successes touched off a wave of insurrection among both tribes."[13]

The British attempted to consolidate their gains in the Khyber Pass by building a series of permanent *piquets* to protect the route through the corridor. G.N. Molesworth, a British officer serving on the frontier in this period, left an interesting account of how one of the largest *piquets* was constructed and of the fighting techniques of the Pashtun tribesmen:

> This *piquet* was built to contain 100 rifles, one of the largest built on the Frontier. We always garrisoned it and worked on improving it continuously during the months to come. In its final form, it was like a long [and] shallow oval with blunted ends. The stone breastwork was some [four to six feet] high to enable a rifleman to fire over it standing and about two to three feet thick. Large stones were placed on the parapet at intervals, like almonds on a tipsy-cake, and loopholes were constructed at ground

level. It was a tribal custom when attacking a *piquet* by day or night, to divide into a rifle party and a knife party. The rifle party kept the heads of the defenders down, while the knife party crept up and jumped over the parapet to start a "free-for-all," often with success. The ground-level loopholes frustrated this amiable tactic.[14]

According to Molesworth, small bastions were built at each end of the *piquet* designed to house machineguns that could provide flanking fire. In the center of the position, the soldiers located the command post, supplies, first aid station, and kitchen. At a later stage, barbed wire and a landline telephone were added.[15]

Even with these formidable outposts and the commitment of a British infantry brigade to protect their lines of communication, the Afridis were able to carry out sniper attacks, sever telephone lines, build roadblocks and ambush convoys along the road. As the British prepared to conduct punitive expeditions, large *lashkars* began forming in the adjacent hills. To make matters worse, tribal militia units began deserting. Taking their guns and ammunition with them. Many Afridis belonging to the famed Khyber Rifles joined their fellow tribesmen in the hills. To the south of the Khyber Pass, the Afghan offensive continued.[16]

By the third week in May, Afghan regular army units had penetrated into Waziristan where they received support from the Mahsuds and Wazirs. According to British military historian Brian Robson; "The British strategy for Waziristan was to maintain an active defence within the resources available, if necessary abandoning temporarily the westernmost Militia posts in the Tochi and Gomal Valleys."[17] In the Tochi Valley, Pashtun militiamen occupying several posts mutinied. Shortly thereafter, in South Waziristan, Afridi and Wazir officers and soldiers also mutinied, forcing the remaining British and Indian forces into headlong retreat back to Mir Ali. "The 1,100 deserters seized 1,190 rifles and over 700,000 rounds of ammunition from their posts which were then employed with deadly effect against imperial troops;" wrote Moreman.[18]

By the 27th of May in 1919, Afghan forces, in conjunction with their Pashtun brethren, surrounded the British encampment at Thal. British Brigadier General Reginald Dyer, a solid veteran of tribal warfare, hastily moved south from the Khyber region with a relief column and sent the Afghan army into a hurried retreat. Dyer hounded the retreating Afghan forces with aircraft, armored vehicles, and cavalry. By the first week in June, the Afghans had had enough and an armistice was signed, effectively ending the Third Afghan War. In an effort to punish the Wazirs, the British attacked a Wazir village south of Thal, destroying fortifications and taking away grain and livestock. However, these punitive expeditions had little effect. As the summer wore on, the Pashtun tribes continued to form *lashkars* and attack British and Indian forces. "On 17th July 1919," wrote Moreman; "the Khyber Pass was closed when 10,000 tribesmen gathered in the Bazar Valley and attacked *piquets* between Bagiari and Ali Musjid. Barley Hill *piquet* was captured the following day by Afridi tribesmen and deserters still wearing khaki uniforms who carried out a carefully implemented assault under the cover of intense rifle fire, demonstrating the growing sophistication of tribal tactics."[19]

The new Pashtun expertise resulted from skilled soldiers, well versed in modern tactics, deserting from the British ranks, and the acquisition by many tribesmen of high velocity rifles which used smokeless powder. Sir Andrew Skeen, a British general who played a vital role in the campaign, described the impact of the new tactics and the high velocity rifle in his book *Passing it On: Short Talks on Tribal Fighting on the North-West Frontier of India:*

> The greatest change so far in tribal methods and in steps needed to counter them has been brought about by the high velocity rifle and by smokeless powder. The first has, of course, added to the tribesmen's power for harm but it has done more than that. It has made every valley into a "Tangi," or defile, and in place of *piquets* covering the close vicinity of columns on the move or in camp, we now have to hold the heights at any distance up to fifteen hundred yards and more from it. Longer to reach, more loss in taking them, more men to hold them, and harder to get away from. [20]

Skeen offered that the arrival of modern rifles among Pashtun enemies meant that British forces had to slow down. He noted;

> When I started this game, seizing a *piquet* position was a simple thing, taking the time it took to scale some point overlooking the line of march at three hundred yards or so and when you got to it, you hadn't to expect bullets snickering in from far off and from somewhere you couldn't see. Holding it was equally simple, for though sometimes overlooked at the then effective range, it was not practically always overlooked [by the enemy], as at present.[21]

The new technology would force the British to reconsider their tactics.

While the conventional fight with the Afghan Army had gone well for the British, outbreaks of tribal violence continued into the fall of 1919. According to Moreman, from late summer and into the fall; "Mahsud and Wazir raiding gangs, varying between 70 and 600 tribesmen, committed 182 offences in Zhob, the Derajat, and the Punjab, killing 225 British subjects and wounding 276 [as well as] kidnapping and ransoming a further 126 civilians. In the process, large quantities of camels, cattle, and private property were stolen and carried off into the hills."[22] The lack of trained soldiers and skilled frontier fighters greatly enhanced the Pashtuns marauding success.[23] As usual, the British and Indian forces planned to launch retaliatory expeditions against the culprits. However, punitive operations had to be delayed due to the deficiency of trained soldiers. Lord Chelmsford, the British Viceroy, described the reasons for the postponement:

> We have roughly two experienced officers per battalion in the Indian Army. The rest are men of practically no military experience and certainly no frontier war experience. Moreover, the troops on the whole have very short service. The result is that vis-à-vis the Wazir and Mahsud our men are inferior and the officers, through their inexperience, are unable to make up for deficiencies in the rank and file. It was because of this inexperience of our officers and troops that during the recent operations, we had to mass such a large force on our frontier.[24]

The Viceroy, like other contemporary officers, stressed that the type of campaigns on the frontier required dispersed action and that would lead to mistakes among less experienced leaders. He contended; "in the case of tribal operations, the junior officers have to take responsibility for the work, we must expect these setbacks from time to time."[25]

Finally in November, the British were able to assemble a force of over 29,000 soldiers for the planned punitive expedition into Waziristan. Major General Skipton Climo would command the expedition. According to one source; "The size of the force which assembled in the Derajat during the autumn of 1919 was unprecedented, reflecting the serious fighting that was anticipated against the heavily armed local tribesmen in Waziristan and the recognized poor quality of the available manpower."[26] Six infantry brigades along with a large contingent of cavalry, engineers, aircraft from the Royal Air Force, and several mountain batteries, along with a massive combat support element were organized for the offensive. In South Waziristan,

16,000 Mahsuds and 7,000 Wazirs armed with 11,000 rifles waited for the British advance.[27]

By mid-November, two British infantry brigades had moved into the Tochi Valley. For the most part, the Tochi Wazirs put up little resistance. The RAF dropped leaflets on Wazir villages informing villagers that if they did not comply with the terms of the government, the RAF would return with bombs. On the 17th of November, General Climo met with a large Tochi *jirga* and the Tochi Wazirs *maliks* agreed to the government terms. A few noncompliant sub-tribes were swiftly dealt with by the RAF who attacked their villages with 17 aircraft. The next day, the sub-tribes also agreed to the government's terms.[28]

While the British were dealing with the Tochi Wazirs, they were also conducting negotiations with the Mahsuds in southern Waziristan. At a *jirga* conducted at Kirghi on the 11th of November, the Mahsuds, unlike the Tochi Wazirs, steadfastly refused to submit to the government terms. The government's conditions were considered mild but included the building of fortifications on Mahsud territory. Acting swiftly, the RAF launched a series of massive bombing raids on Mahsud villages dropping an average of 10,000 pounds of bombs a day for nine days. The bombing however, had little effect on the tribesmen and considering the *Pashtunwali* code's emphasis on revenge, almost certainly fueled Mahsud intransigence.[29] Thomas H. Johnson and M. Chris Mason have contended that the revenge was so important that; "It may take generations to avenge the wrong but retribution will be the focus of the [Pashtun] family's life until honor is recouped."[30]

Taken as a whole, the air campaign against the tribes had a negligible effect. "Whilst the RAF could be very effective at intimidating wavering tribal sections into making a settlement with the government," wrote historian Alan Warren; "determined *lashkars* learned to cope with air attacks. Insurgents became accustomed to protecting their bases from aerial bombing by siting them in caves."[31] To be sure, the Mahsuds were self confident and certain of success. A British officer would later suggest that the source of Mahsud confidence lay in their knowledge that British forces did not have the proper training and that the aircraft had not delivered a decisive weapon to those forces. This officer further emphasized the role of the British trained tribesmen who had joined up with enemy elements:

> The number of deserters from the Waziristan Militias and of former soldiers of the regular Indian Army who were to be found amongst them, was large. This total has been calculated at over 1,800. Not only would the presence of

these men greatly influence the tactics of the tribesmen in action but their knowledge of the habits and routine of the Indian troops opposed to them would prove of great value and a source of much confidence in the class of warfare in which the tribesmen excelled.[32]

Unable to bring the Mahsud to terms through the use of airpower, the British began planning for ground operations against the tribe. Major General Skeen would command two brigades that would assemble at Jandola and advance into Mahsud territory. The strike force was christened the Derajat Column. Unlike past campaigns, only one column would advance against the enemy. According to Moreman;

> [This] reflected the shortage of transport, the large winter scale of baggage and stores required, the recognised low fighting ability of the raw and untrained regiments available, and the large number of breech-loading rifles in Mahsud hands. A single line of communication also required fewer troops, a smaller number of administrative units, and reduced the demand for transport and supplies to a minimum. Moreover, it was hoped that an advance by a single column would encourage the tribesmen to mass, giving imperial troops an opportunity to inflict a decisive defeat at the outset of the campaign.[33]

Unfortunately for the British, they had greatly underestimated their enemy.

On the 11th of December, as Skeen's two brigades prepared to move, two battalions accompanied by two mountain guns advanced approximately one and a half miles west of Jandola. Their mission was to set up *piquets* on the high ground in order to protect the strike force as it moved into Jandola. Over the course of the next three days, the Mahsuds launched vicious assaults on every small unit they could find, inflicting over 50 casualties on the inexperienced British forces. These attacks caused great consternation within the British command. It was soon determined that any major encampment that was established or any advance by the Derajat column up the Tank Zam would have to be protected by permanent *piquets*. As one British officer later pointed out:

> To protect the valley road, it was therefore proposed to have recourse to the system of permanent *piquets* in preference to the employment of *piquets* temporarily posted day by day as the Striking Force should advance and to

a system of escorts for the protection of subsequent supply columns. These permanent *piquets* were now to be placed at moderately close intervals on all commanding points on either side of the road so that the Striking Force and, in turn, all convoys should be able to move along the valley unattended by any large escort as it were up a corridor, held by garrisoned posts on either flank. All of these posts were to be strongly fortified, surrounded with strong barbed wire entanglements, designed for all around defence, strongly traversed, and supplied with a store of hand grenades or Lewis guns.[34]

The officer underlined the mission of the *piquets* as "the greatest degree of protection obtainable for the valley road at the cost of the smallest number of troops."[35]

By the time Skeen's entire Derajat Column rolled into Jandola on the 17th of December, seven permanent *piquets* had been established on the key terrain surrounding the new encampment. While Skeen surveyed the area, work continued on a few positions above Jandola. Before long, a delegation of Mahsud *maliks* arrived at Jandola to talk with Skeen about immunity for their property which they believed would soon be destroyed by the British forces. At 1530 hours, while Skeen and the *maliks* were still conducting their meeting, a large force of Mahsud fighters attacked a security detail protecting soldiers working on the *piquets* above Jandola. The security detail retreated forthwith and the Mahsuds quickly overran the easternmost *piquet*. "In the face of rifle, Lewis gun, and mountain gun fire," a British officer reported; "the Mahsuds rushed in to close quarters with the utmost recklessness."[36] After killing or wounding 40 men, the Mahsuds were finally forced back, leaving behind 20 lifeless fighters on the hillside. The same British officer concluded that the attack emphasized the prevalent lack of experience of the troops in this class of warfare.[37]

Undeterred by the ferocious Mahsud assaults, Skeen began his advance on the 18th of December. Advancing with his 67th Infantry Brigade, two mountain batteries, the 2d Battalion, 19th Punjabis (2/19), a company of sappers and miners, and a battalion of Sikh pioneers, Skeen marched his column past the intersection of the Shahur and Tank Zam Rivers and soon emerged on the Plain of Palosina.

Here, Skeen halted his column in preparation for building an encampment and placing permanent *piquets* in the hillsides and along his communications lines. Seven airplanes swept the area for signs of the enemy. Initially, the aircraft spotted Mahsud fighters moving up the valley but the

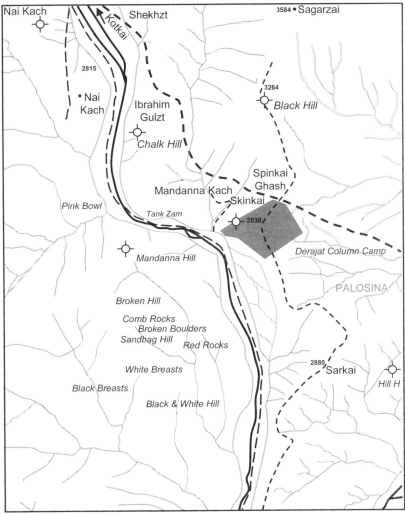

Map 4. The Derajat Encampment.

lashkar quickly broke into small bands and the pilots lost sight of their prey.[38]

The next day, Skeen's soldiers set out to capture the key terrain surrounding Palosina and begin building permanent *piquets*. The British general planned to capture one hill at a time and then build a permanent *piquet* on each one. The first hill on the list was Mandanna Hill and the assignment fell to the 1st Battalion of the 103d Mahrattas Light Infantry (1/103) and the 1st Battalion of the 55th Rifles (1/55). Their artillery fire quickly cleared a group of Mahsud fighters out of a nearby ravine as the Mahrattas made their way up to "Red Rocks" and "Sandbag Hill." At the same time, the 1/55th Rifles supporting the left flank of the Mahrattas occupied "Broken Boulders" and the lower portion of "Sandbag Hill." With these locations secured, the Mahrattas were ordered to secure "Comb Rocks." At this point, reconnaissance flights by the accompanying aircraft failed to spot additional Mahsud fighters and a ground reconnaissance of "Comb Rocks" according to one British source, was deemed "inadequate."[39]

As the Mahrattas made their way over the broken terrain toward their new objective, Mahsud fighters opened a substantial and deadly converging fire from "Comb Rocks." The rifle fire stopped the Mahrattas in their tracks. Even with the support of the prepositioned artillery, the 1/103d failed to capture the position and suffered devastating casualties. "So fully were the Mahsuds alive to the value of their improved armament that no black powder weapons were allowed into the fight by day and their application of fire was carefully organized;" Skeen would later declare. "The use of long range sniping and covering fire from all ranges," he stated "was designed to let the swordsmen close."[40]

As the Mahrattas began to waver, the Mahsuds launched a massive and well coordinated counterattack which swept the 1/103d from Sandbag Hill. Using well directed covering fire from the summit, the Mahsuds shot down the flanking companies of the Mahrattas causing a complete rout. As the soldiers from the 1/103d fell back, they ran through a company of the 1/55th Rifles triggering great alarm in the ranks. In short order, the Mahsuds, numbering about 900 fighters, drove both battalions back toward Palosina. According to one British source; "The British casualties amounted to some 250, whilst 130 rifles and 10 Lewis guns were lost. The fall of their commanding officer early in the day followed by that of four other British officers, had left the 103d virtually helpless. Moreover, the behavior of the men also showed that they had lost all confidence in themselves and all control of their weapons. The Mahrattas had kept no reserve and their small supports were inadequate to control the retreat."[41] A few British officers also blamed the disaster on a lack of air support. So complete was the mad dash down the hillside that the day became known as "Derby Day" by those who witnessed the event.[42]

On the next day, Skeen threw in four battalions and all of his artillery and aircraft to capture Mandanna Hill. This time there was no opposition from the Mahsud and the British quickly began building a *piquet* on the hilltop. However, as the covering force withdrew from Mandanna Hill, the Mahsud struck the incomplete fortification along with the 110 defenders from the 2/19 Punjabis, sending them scurrying back towards Palosina. Moreman noted that; "The demoralized survivors—abandoning rifles,

Lewis guns, Mills bombs, and other equipment—frantically withdrew to the safety of the perimeter camp in the valley below pursued by a Mahsud force under half their strength."[43]

Skeen now decided to change direction and attempt to re-establish his force's shattered morale. Bringing up the 67th Brigade under the command of Brigadier General F.G. Lucas, the British quickly occupied "Black Hill" north of Palosina and began constructing a *piquet* on the 21st of December. In the early afternoon, the Mahsuds struck again with approximately 1,000 fighters. Covering fire from up to 1,500 yards away allowed Mahsud swordsmen to overrun the security detachment and close in on the Sikhs inside the p*iquet*. Although the 3/24th Sikh Pioneers put up a gallant struggle, they were soon forced to retreat. While Skeen's artillery was able to adjust fire on the throng of tribesmen, killing 250 and wounding 300, British casualties totaled over 300 soldiers. Bolstered by the success of their artillery, the British counterattacked up "Black Hill" but were soon forced back by the highly accurate fire from well masked Mahsud riflemen.[44]

Thus far in the campaign, the British and Indian forces had proven no match for the Mahsud. On the 30th of December, Skeen offered his assessment to his superiors regarding the debacle:

> The actions last week have given some valuable lessons which will be of immediate interest and importance. Those operations have shown the vital necessity of regaining some standard of musketry efficiency. Marksmanship and fire discipline are two of the first essentials in frontier fighting and the present Indian Army as a general rule has never learnt these arts. The result is that as the men have no faith in their rifles, they have little self confidence and look to auxiliaries such as artillery, aeroplanes, and Lewis guns for their protection and to win the battle. In this connection, it may be remarked that practically none of the junior British officers have had experience of hill warfare and experience of warfare against a civilized and organised enemy is not necessarily good training for hill warfare against a savage enemy.[45]

Skeen concluded; "Nothing can replace these arts and frontier warfare must remain expensive on lives and rich in unpleasant incidents until our infantry regains some of its ancient knowledge of musketry and fire discipline and so get renewed confidence in themselves and in their weapons."[46]

Skeen's assessment was correct. However, he failed to mention the former Mahsud soldiers and militiamen who had deserted and who now bolstered the ranks of the *lashkars*. According to one source "These men formed one-fifth to one-sixth of the Mahsud fighting strength— approximately 2,000 men— encountered during the initial phase of the campaign, providing *lashkars* with leadership, discipline, and tactical training that they had always lacked before in Waziristan."[47] British Lieutenant Colonel Herman de Watteville also concluded; "Much of the newly found skill may be attributed to the presence in their ranks of ex-officers and many hundreds of ex-privates of the Waziristan Militia and of the regular Indian infantry."[48]

Fortunately for the British and Indian forces, heavy casualties and a shortage of supplies forced the Mahsud *lashkars* to disband on the 21st of December. This respite allowed Skeen's command to finish building their permanent *piquets* around Palosina and along their communication lines. It had been a close call for the British. In fact, the prospect of defeat loomed so large that Skeen and Climo had called for reinforcements and for the use of poison gas. While their request for poison gas was rejected, reinforcements consisting of two Gurkha battalions were quickly rushed to Waziristan. On the 28th of December, Skeen began his new offensive up the Tank Zam Valley. Bad weather, horrific terrain, the lack of trained soldiers, and continued resistance from the Mahsuds forced Skeen to rely heavily on his air and artillery assets and the permanent *piquet* system. Until the first week of January in 1920, Skeen's command was unable to advance more than four miles a day.[49]

British and Indian spirits soon began to improve as the Gurkha battalions and veteran British officers started to arrive at the front and unreliable units were pulled out of the line. Fierce combat continued from the 9th of January to the 15th. On the 14th of January alone, the British suffered 450 casualties in fighting in and around Ahnai Tangi. During this period the British and Indian forces had some success in conducting night attacks against the Mahsud. As an example, Skeen's forces captured the Barari Tangi gorge on the 28th of January in a successful night assault. "Night operations," wrote Moreman; "were now regularly employed to seize *piquets*, jumping off areas, and important defensive positions during five of the larger operations. These avoided heavy casualties, extended operations outside daylight hours, and often forestalled the tribesmen occupying and defending strong positions and thereby using their rifles to full effect."[50] New *lashkars* that had assembled to launch counterattacks in the Barari Tangi gorge area were pummeled by artillery and the RAF causing them to retreat into the hills. At this point, tribal morale plummeted and as one British historian suggested; "There were definite limits to the amount of punishment an irregular tribal force could withstand."[51]

By mid-February, the Derajat column had penetrated into Mahsud country and Skeen's engineers began punitive operations in the Makin Valley. Over 451 Mahsud structures were destroyed. In March, a second round of punitive operations was launched in the vicinity of Kaniguram. While the tribesmen continued to snipe at the British and Indian forces conducting the reprisals, it was clearly evident that the Mahsud had reached their limit of endurance.[52]

By early April, active operations were over and Skeen's command built a permanent camp near Ladha. Alan Warren observed; "One advantage of the Ladha camp was that it was within six-inch howitzer range of Makin, meaning that future bad behavior by the residents of that area would be speedily punished."[53] As the British official history of the campaign pointed out however; "It was impossible to force this tribe of unruly and obdurate individuals, recognizing no responsible leaders and no form of organized government, to make any engagements or to keep such promises if made, once the troops had left the country."[54] Indeed, even after terms were settled upon with some tribal sections, raids and attacks continued from Mahsud sanctuaries in Afghanistan. It would take until November of 1920 to reoccupy all the posts formerly in British hands.[55]

It had been a costly campaign for the British. From December of 1919 until April of 1920, their forces suffered 2,286 dead, wounded, and missing. As a British historian noted; "This represented the highest 'butcher's bill' ever suffered during operations against the trans-border Pathan tribes."[56] General Monro, the Commander-in-Chief, was convinced that the operations;

> have merely borne out the principles of mountain warfare, which are well known from former campaigns. It is necessary here however, to lay emphasis upon the supreme importance of adequate training of troops prior to their employment in a mountain campaign. Nothing can take the place of careful individual training. If possible, it is more essential in mountain warfare then in any other class of fighting that troops should have confidence in their weapons. This can only be obtained by systematic individual training which must include instructions in making the best tactical use of the ground, in principles of fire and movement, and the mental development of the soldier to

such a degree of alertness that no target escapes from detection and appropriate action is immediately taken.[57]

Once again, the British Commander-in-Chief's assessment was accurate but failed to mention the superior performance of the enemy. As de Watteville would later suggest; "The opening days of the campaign found the Mahsuds in a state of elation and of determination hitherto unknown on the Frontier. Their armament had improved, their supply of ammunition was large while their tactical conceptions had made enormous strides."[58] These tactical conceptions were brought about by trained Pashtuns who fled the British ranks and joined their brethren in the holy war against the infidel. Not only were these deserters well versed in modern tactics, they were able to train their fellow fighters in an astoundingly short period of time and nearly overwhelm the British at Palosina. As the British experience demonstrated, training of the indigenous population in military tactics and techniques, although necessary, can become a liability.

At the conclusion of the major fighting in Waziristan, the Indian Army once again began retraining its forces to conduct trans-border or hill warfare. As in the aftermath of the Tirah campaign, the British set about writing new training manuals and instituting new training programs to ensure that all soldiers confronting the Pashtuns on the North-West Frontier were properly trained. Part of the new British military pacification program included the building of new roads into Waziristan and the stationing of British and Indian soldiers close to Mahsud territory. These new all weather roads would allow the military to move rapidly into the region. However, the construction of the new roads would set the stage for further conflict in Waziristan.[59]

Notes

1.   T.R. Moreman, "'Passing It On:' The Army in India and Frontier Warfare, 1914–39," in *War and Society in Colonial India* edited by Kaushik Roy (Oxford, UK: Oxford University Press, 2006), 277–278.

2.   Jules Stewart, *The Khyber Rifles: From the British Raj to Al Qaeda* (Phoenix Mill, UK: Sutton Publishing Limited, 2005), 167–168; T.R. Moreman, *The Army in India and the Development of Frontier Warfare, 1849–1947* (London: Macmillan Press Ltd., 1998), 91–92.

3.   Stewart, 167–168

4.   Quoted in T.R. Moreman, *The Army in India and the Development of Frontier Warfare, 1849–1947*, 92.

5.   T.R. Moreman, *The Army in India and the Development of Frontier Warfare, 1849–1947*, 92.

6.   T.R. Moreman, "'Passing It On:' The Army in India and Frontier Warfare, 1914–39," 278.

7.   T.R. Moreman, "'Passing It On:' The Army in India and Frontier Warfare, 1914–39," 278.

8.   T.R. Moreman, "'Passing It On:' The Army in India and Frontier Warfare, 1914–39," 279.

9.   Alan Warren, *Waziristan, the Faqir of Ipi and the Indian Army: The North-West Frontier Revolt of 1936–1937* (Oxford, UK: Oxford University Press, 2000), 37.

10.   Quoted in H. de Watteville, *Waziristan, 1919–1920*, Campaigns and Their Lessons Series (London: Constable and Co. Ltd, 1925), 5.

11.   Quoted in Brian Robson, *Crisis on the Frontier: The Third Afghan War and the Campaign in Waziristan 1919–1920* (Staplehurst, UK: Spellmount, 2004), xi.

12.   T.R. Moreman, *The Army in India and the Development of Frontier Warfare, 1849–1947*, 103; Robson, xi, 43.

13.   Robson, 83.

14.   Lieutenant General G.N. Molesworth, *Afghanistan 1919: An Account of Operations in the Third Afghan War* (New York: Asia Publishing House, 1962), 73.

15.   Lieutenant General G.N. Molesworth, *Afghanistan 1919: An Account of Operations in the Third Afghan War* (New York: Asia Publishing House, 1962), 73.

16.   T.R. Moreman, *The Army in India and the Development of Frontier Warfare, 1849–1947*, 104; Robson, 83.

17.   Robson, 165.

18.   T.R. Moreman, *The Army in India and the Development of Frontier Warfare, 1849–1947*, 104.

19.   T.R. Moreman, *The Army in India and the Development of Frontier Warfare, 1849–1947*, 105–106.

20. General Sir Andrew Skeen, *Passing It On: Short Talks on the Tribal Fighting on the North-West Frontier of India* (London: Gale and Polden, 1932), 12–13.

21. General Sir Andrew Skeen, *Passing It On: Short Talks on the Tribal Fighting on the North-West Frontier of India* (London: Gale and Polden, 1932), 12–13.

22. T.R. Moreman, *The Army in India and the Development of Frontier Warfare, 1849–1947*, 107.

23. de Watteville, 64. de Watteville listed the misdeeds as follows: "Tochi Wazirs: Fifty raids and various offences resulting in British-Indian casualties: 30 killed, 60 wounded, 5 missing; also a large quantity of loot in the shape of cattle, stores and money. Mahsuds: Over 100 raids and various offences resulting in British-Indian casualties: 135 killed, 100 wounded, 38 missing; also loot to the extent of 448 camels, 1674 cattle and property to the value of Rs. 35,000. Wana Wazirs: Thirty-two raids and various offences resulting in British-Indian casualties: 55 killed, 106 wounded, 83 missing; also a large quantity of loot, including camels and cattle."

24. Quoted in T.R. Moreman, *The Army in India and the Development of Frontier Warfare, 1849–1947*, 106–107.

25. Quoted in T.R. Moreman, *The Army in India and the Development of Frontier Warfare, 1849–1947*, 106–107.

26. T.R. Moreman, *The Army in India and the Development of Frontier Warfare, 1849–1947*, 107.

27. Warren, 285.

28. de Watteville, 80–81; Warren, 45.

29. de Watteville, 82; T.R. Moreman, *The Army in India and the Development of Frontier Warfare, 1849–1947*, 108; Warren, 45–46.

30. Thomas H. Johnson and M. Chris Mason, "No Sign until the Burst of Fire: Understanding the Pakistan-Afghanistan Frontier," *International Security*, Vol. 32, No.4 (Spring 2008), 63.

31. Warren, 285.

32. de Watteville, 65–66.

33. T.R. Moreman, *The Army in India and the Development of Frontier Warfare, 1849–1947*, 108.

34. de Watteville, 98–99.

35. de Watteville, 98–99.

36. de Watteville, 99.

37. de Watteville, 99–100.

38. de Watteville, 101; Warren, 46; T.R. Moreman, *The Army in India and the Development of Frontier Warfare, 1849–1947*, 108.

39. de Watteville, 104.

40. Skeen, 14.

41. de Watteville, 104–105.

42. T.R. Moreman, *The Army in India and the Development of Frontier Warfare, 1849–1947*, 108–109.

43. T.R. Moreman, *The Army in India and the Development of Frontier Warfare, 1849–1947*, 109.

44. T.R. Moreman, *The Army in India and the Development of Frontier Warfare, 1849–1947*, 109; de Watteville, 108–109.

45. Quoted in T.R. Moreman, *The Army in India and the Development of Frontier Warfare, 1849–1947*, 112.

46. Quoted in T.R. Moreman, *The Army in India and the Development of Frontier Warfare, 1849–1947*, 112.

47. Quoted in T.R. Moreman, *The Army in India and the Development of Frontier Warfare, 1849–1947*, 111.

48. de Watteville, 114–115.

49. T.R. Moreman, *The Army in India and the Development of Frontier Warfare, 1849–1947*, 111–113;

50. T.R. Moreman, *The Army in India and the Development of Frontier Warfare, 1849–1947*, 119.

51. Warren, 49.

52. Warren, 49; T.R. Moreman, *The Army in India and the Development of Frontier Warfare, 1849–1947*, 119–120.

53. Warren, 49–50.

54. Quoted in Warren, 49.

55. T.R. Moreman, *The Army in India and the Development of Frontier Warfare, 1849–1947*, 119–120.

56. T.R. Moreman, *The Army in India and the Development of Frontier Warfare, 1849–1947*, 120.

57. Quoted in T.R. Moreman, *The Army in India and the Development of Frontier Warfare, 1849–1947*, 120–121.

58. de Watteville, 222.

59. Warren, 53–55.

Chapter 4

British Military Operations on the North-West Frontier
1921–1947

The tribesman will never believe that passivity is due to
anything but fear and weakness.

Colonel S.F. Muspratt

The leading consideration is to deny to the enemy, the most
important points from which he can bring effective fire to
bear. This is a precaution which must never be neglected,
even when the country is to all appearance, unoccupied.

Manual of Operations on the North-West Frontier
Army Headquarters, India, 1925

From 1920 to 1924, British and Indian forces in Waziristan continued
to battle the tribes in what has been described as a low intensity campaign.
The persistent combat as well as a new training program, greatly enhanced
the fighting ability of British and Indian soldiers on the North-West Frontier. During this time, some British officers also sought to introduce new
more lethal weapons systems to the North-West Frontier such as poison
gas. A few British officers however, remained skeptical of these new weapons, fearing their extreme effects. In 1923, British Colonel Frederick Keen
wrote that; "We should realize, as we have perhaps not done in the past,
that in fighting the Pathans we are engaging in civil war and that it is to
our advantage that enemies of today should be turned into our friends of
tomorrow. In a word, our coercive measures should always be directed
with a view to eventual pacification and control."[1] Although Keen's assessment was more enlightened than that of many of his fellow officers, it
certainly did not reflect most counter-insurgency doctrine of the early 21st
century. In fact, in his 1925 publication *Letters of a Once Punjab Frontier
Force Officer to his Nephew*, British Colonel J.P. Villiers-Stuart captured
the views of the majority of the British officers on the North-West Frontier.
"In operating against tribesmen we have two objects in view;" he wrote to
his nephew. "Emphatically to kill as many as possible. That being by far
the most convincing form of argument," and, he concluded, "To destroy
his villages and stores of food and capture his cattle and sheep."[2] It was
the tried and true British method of dealing with the Pashtuns, a strategy
designed to inflict quick and decisive punishment and to bring the errant
tribes back into line as quickly as possible. This approach however, significantly increased the Pashtuns desire for revenge. While countless British

officers were familiar with the Pashtun code of *Pashtunwali,* they seem to have never fully grasped the fact that their punitive operations against the tribes only increased the Pashtun fervor for settling old scores. It was an error of assessment that would play a major role in the continued reciprocal violence on the North-West Frontier.

While the British Army in India remained steadfast in its strategic and operational approach to the Pashtuns, it was determined after the near de-bacle of the 1919–1920 campaign, to regain its tactical prowess on the North-West Frontier. In 1925, the British army published the *Manual of Operations on the North-West Frontier of India* and distributed 35,000 copies to its soldiers. According to British historian T.R. Moreman, the new manual reflected the important changes that had occurred in frontier warfare since the First World War. Its pages reflected the Indian Army's extensive experience of military operations against the trans-border Pathan tribes and brought up to date the existing doctrine and system of training caused by improved tribal tactics, leadership and equipment, and changes in the organization, training, and equipment of imperial troops.[3] The document proved highly instructive for both British and Indian soldiers on the frontier and although filled with the usual early 20th century British hyperbole, retains its relevance for military forces operating in the region in the early 21st century.

In reference to the Pashtuns, the new *Manual of Operations* stated that the tribes were formidable when attacking a detachment isolated beyond reach of support and were adept in all arts of individual warfare, always seeking and seldom missing an opportunity.[4] Indeed, attacks on small remote US combat outposts in Afghanistan between 2002 and 2009 reveal that little has changed. The *Manual of Operations* also concluded that; "In all movements involving a subsequent withdrawal such as reconnaissances, foraging, etc., no defile through which the troops will have to pass in returning and no commanding point from which the enemy could harass the withdrawal, should be left unguarded."[5] The instruction manual also pointed out that all outposts or camps should be protected by *piquets* in order to deny the enemy commanding ground from which to bring effective fire to bear on the camp by day or night.[6] While securing the high ground above a combat outpost or camp would seem to be an obvious necessity and time honored tactic, it is one that the British periodically failed to incorporate.

In confronting the Pashtuns, British and Indian soldiers learned early on that they could not wait for multiple intelligence reports or for patterns to develop before securing or reinforcing a camp, as the enemy was always prepared to strike a poorly defended or isolated detachment. "They will attack readily if they see a chance and when they do, they make very clever use of covering fire;" wrote Colonel Villiers-Stuart. "They also occasionally put in very determined charges, covered by rifle fire, either day or night. They always come suddenly. It may sound odd that such charges can succeed, but I have myself seen a party of fifteen men of a thoroughly good regiment cut up with swords and knives in broad daylight. So it can happen."[6] As the British yet again learned, camps or combat outposts had to be protected by securing the surrounding high ground. To be sure, by 1925, British and Indian officers were well aware that the first step in establishing a new camp was to send parties up to seize the commanding ground.[7]

From 1925 to 1930, units stationed in the North-West Frontier continued to train in mountain warfare using the *Manual of Operations on the North-West Frontier of India* as their guide. During this period, a heated debate arose among British officers. Many were convinced that the Army in India spent too much time focusing on mountain or "savage warfare" and not enough time focusing on conventional warfare. A veteran British officer summed up the debate in a professional journal; "There are two forms of warfare to be taught in India, open warfare and mountain warfare. Except for those stationed on the frontier, the former of course requires the most attention but mountain warfare should never be entirely neglected in view of the fact that whenever the Army of India fights in the future it is almost certain to be in mountainous country."[8]

While this debate raged on in the professional journals, the Army in India was rapidly becoming more mechanized. The new road networks constructed within the North-West Frontier, particularly in Waziristan, allowed trucks, armored cars, and light tanks to move swiftly up and down the valley floors. According to Moreman, this; "clearly altered the strategic, tactical, and administrative conduct of frontier warfare, enabling reinforcements to be rushed to the threatened points along the border."[9] This newfound mobility however, created many unforeseen problems. More soldiers were now required in supporting roles and the logistical tail of the columns increased considerably. However, congested avenues of approach and lines of communication could be easily observed by the Pashtuns. Additionally, a company of Vickers medium machine guns was added to each battalion while the number of riflemen in the battalion was decreased. This caused a reduction in *piquets* employed to guard against surprise and greatly increased the column of pack animals needed to convey the extra equipment.

In short, the mechanization and modernization of the British Army in India, at least initially, produced a force both cumbersome and self-assured. These attributes were ill advised when fighting the Pashtuns in the mountains of the North-West Frontier. Not surprisingly, tactical off-road mobility suffered and any column advancing along the valley floors slowed significantly due the increased use of pack animals. "In the early 1930s a certain complacency about the Frontier became discernible;" wrote a British veteran of the North-West Frontier. "An almost reluctant belief that with planes, light armor, improved mountain artillery, a higher scale of light machine guns, the scales were so heavily weighted against him that the poor Pathan would be reduced to a little long range sniping. The events of the next decade were to correct these ideas. Keen young officers who were disappointed that the Frontier was not all it was cracked up to be, discovered that indeed it was."[10]

The British Army in India was greatly embarrassed when far reaching tribal violence erupted in the summer of 1930. Tribal *lashkars* successfully penetrated into the Peshawar District and vanished back into the mountains with little loss. The ensuing campaign produced a firestorm of derision from the press and both political and military communities. Moreman cited many of the problems associated with this campaign:

> The additional machine guns dramatically increased the firepower making *lashkars* wary of engaging Indian columns or following up rear guards thereby limiting opportunities to inflict heavy casualties. Further problems were caused by an obsession with security that overrode other operational requirements, slowed movement to a crawl, and tied Indian columns to cautious and unimaginative advances along the valley floors. It now took longer to picket a route as periodic halts were necessary while covering machine gun and artillery fire was carefully arranged to support the placement and withdrawal of pickets. Fear of casualties, recovery of the dead and wounded, and efforts to prevent the theft of arms and ammunition also stultified efforts to bring hostile *lashkars* to battle or to achieve surprise. An inability to differentiate between the tactical requirements of conventional warfare and those of the frontier compounded the problems.[11]

To its credit, the Army in India took immediate steps to rectify the problems. The first priority was to build more roads in the North-West Frontier in order to increase mobility. While this project proved effective, it also triggered violent clashes with many of the Pashtun tribes who vehemently objected to the new road building projects. "Henceforth," wrote Moreman; "punitive operations in tribal territory were normally combined with road construction to allow small lightly-equipped columns to be supplied and to operate in the hills as well as extending political control."[12]

Other measures adopted by the high command included reducing the load of the infantry in order to increase both their off road mobility and the time spent establishing *piquets*. The number of pack animals used for punitive operations was also greatly curtailed. New training initiatives were quickly adopted while many experienced veteran frontier officers and non-commissioned officers (NCOs) were placed into the regimental ranks.[13]

Perhaps one of the most important developments was General Andrew Skeen's 1932 unofficial publication *Passing it On: Short Talks on Tribal Fighting on the North-West Frontier of India*. Skeen was widely considered the most experienced frontier officer in the British Army. His book contained a wealth of information on the Pashtuns and advice regarding how to conduct tactical operations against them. The work proved so instructive that it was distributed to both officers and NCOs. The book's lessons have proven so durable that a Pakistani press reprinted it in 2009 under the new title *Tribal Fighting in NWFP*.[14]

By 1935, the British and Indian forces on the North-West Frontier had made great strides. New roads into tribal territories increased mobility while the reduction of light infantry loads further improved the army's off-road capabilities. New training manuals and unofficial publications greatly enhanced the soldier's knowledge of the enemy and the tactical expertise required to defeat him. However, in the late summer of 1935, further road construction into Mohmand tribal land and anti-British agitation incited by a local *Faqir* or holy man ignited yet another war which would test the new training and equipment of the Army in India.[15]

Operations Against the Mohmand, 1935

Druing the night of 14-15 August 1935, a Mohmand *lashkar* of approximately 1,400 fighters descended on the newly constructed Gandab road and began to destroy it. On the morning of 15 August as the enemy *lashkar* continued to dismantle the highway, a small tribal levy of *Khassadars* who had been paid by the British to protect the road, quickly retreated from the area. While the British hurriedly alerted a brigade column in Peshawar to move against the tribal fighters, the British High Command ordered the RAF to bomb the *lashkar* along the Gandab road. In a departure from previous punitive actions, British political officers ordered the RAF not to bomb nearby villages. However, as additional reinforcements began arriving from two other tribal *khels*, the RAF was authorized to conduct air operations against their villages and, as the official order stated; "Bomb any persons and livestock seen in those areas."[16]

With an eye toward ultimate conciliation, efforts were made to limit these coercive procedures. Royal Air Force pilots were instructed; "This aim was to be attained with the minimum of casualties to the tribesmen and without more material damage than was necessary to compel evacuation."[17] Leaflets were dropped on villages warning the inhabitants of the impending bombing and a demonstration of 38 aircraft flew over the area in hopes of intimidating the tribes. In the end, the RAF bombing did cause some fighters to leave the *lashkar*. Many of the tribesmen quickly left in order to move their families and livestock to safety. As the official history reported however, the bombing did not secure the submission of the hostiles and it was evident that air action alone was unlikely to secure all the objects desired by the government.[18] A warning order was soon issued for three brigades to advance. "Mohforce" as the command was designated, was ordered to remove the tribesmen from the Gandab road and to provide protection for the continued construction of the highway.

The commander of Mohforce, Brigadier C.J.E. Auchinleck, wasted little time in moving his forces into Mohmand country. Although the heat and humidity were stifling, Auchinleck's command pushed into the tribal territory quickly and with great proficiency. Employing light infantry, light tanks, cavalry, and artillery, the British and Indian forces were able to advance with several columns in the face of determined Mohmand resistance. Night movements and the addition of light tanks as part of the constituent field force played a key role in the swiftness of the advance and the battering inflicted on the enemy.[19]

As the official history of these operations pointed out; "the Mohmand Force made full use of movement by night and were thus able to extend their radius of action to round up hostile bodies and to effect surprise by seizing and occupying essential tactical features before it was light."[20] Indeed, two of Auchinleck's brigades were able to conduct a simultaneous night movement to capture the heavily defended high ground around the Nahakki Pass on the 18th of September.

Mohforce also made extensive use of its light tanks which aided the infantry in establishing *piquets* by silencing enemy fire and blasting through Mohmand positions from both flank and rear. In short, according to the official record, the tanks made;

> full use of their mobility and invulnerability against rifle fire [and] established fixed machine gun posts in rear of the general line held by the tribesmen thereby threatening their normal line of retreat and forcing them to withdrawal to the flank. In this way, opposition offered to a direct advance by our infantry was reduced . . . In the withdrawal, tanks accompanied the rear party where possible [and] covered with their fire, the withdrawal of *piquets* by pinning the tribesmen to their ground. On more than one occasion, the mere presence of tanks in a valley was sufficient to deter the tribesmen from following up.[21]

Even before this campaign, General Skeen made it clear that he would hate to be without armoured vehicles anywhere where they could be used.[22]

By September of 1935, Auchinleck had inflicted enough punishment on the Mohmand tribesmen to persuade their leaders to call for *jirgas* and come to terms with the British. In a training memorandum produced by the General Staff, senior British officers concluded;

> The recent Mohmand operations showed marked advance in the conduct of operations of this nature and the methods employed. Apart from the advantages of a L. of C. [Line of Communications] with a road for M.T., [Motor Transport] which was effectively maintained and of efficient administrative arrangements, the rapid and complete success obtained in this campaign may be attributed to enterprising leadership, development of existing methods, and the introduction of innovations.[23]

British and Indian soldiers learned well from the successful tactics used during the campaign. Soon, they expanded their training in night fighting, the employment of tanks, securing lines of communications, and air-land coordination. As they continued to train, violence once again erupted on a grand scale in Waziristan.[24]

The *Faqir* of Ipi and the 1936–1937 Waziristan Campaign

In early 1936, a Pashtun schoolteacher married a young Hindu girl who went by the name of Islam Bibi. She converted to Islam and soon after, the family of the young girl charged the schoolteacher with kidnapping. The case was quickly brought before a magistrate. The issue probably could have been quietly settled by a British political officer and a Waziri *jirga* but by the time the legal action went to court it had gained a great deal of public notoriety. When the magistrate handed down a decision taking the girl away from her Pashtun husband, many Wazirs were convinced that British law had sided with the Hindus. Although British political officers attempted to calm the tribes by engaging in numerous *jirgas*, the situation quickly spiraled out of control. In Waziristan in Tori *Khel* country, a large *lashkar* began to form led by a cunning religious zealot known as the *Faqir* of Ipi.[25]

According to the historian Arthur Swinson, the *Faqir* of Ipi, whose real name was Mirza Ali Khan, was a man who; "could be brutal and treacherous even by Pathan standards. He took bribes, he sheltered outlaws, he was not above hiring assassins to deal with his enemies, and even his enemies' children."[26] The *Faqir* of Ipi used the Islam Bibi case to stir up the tribesmen and advocate a new holy war against the infidel. In Tori *Khel* country, the *Faqir* of Ipi managed to incite many of the more volatile tribesmen, many of whom welcomed a chance to fight the British once more. Loyal *maliks* or elders in the region convinced the Government of India that a visit by British and Indian soldiers into Tori *Khel* country would probably encourage the tribe to expel the *Faqir* of Ipi. Unfortunately, this "peaceful demonstration" as the British official history called it, would stir up a hornet's nest and plunge most of Waziristan into turmoil.[27]

On the 25th of November in 1936, two brigade-sized columns began a synchronized move into Tori *Khel* country. The Razmak Column (Razcol) would move from Damdil while the Tochi Column (Tocol) advanced from Mir Ali. Both columns were to converge at Biche Kashkai and then return to their starting locations. The British official history reported; "It was hoped that this move would strengthen the hands of the local *maliks* and check the *Faqir*'s propaganda. The attitude of the Tori *Khel* as a whole seemed satisfactory and serious opposition was not anticipated. The troops, therefore, were to carry out what was purely a peaceful demonstration on a timed programme and were to take no offensive action unless forced to retaliate in their own defence."[28] Since this was a peacetime operation, British commanders saw no need for a well defended line of communication. In fact, no logistical arrangements were made at all.

Razcol soon ran into stiff tribal resistance on the outskirts of Biche Kashkai. Although "close *piquets*" were used along the route, 14 soldiers had been killed and 43 wounded by the time the column made its way into Biche Kashkai. While Razcol went to work constructing a perimeter camp at Biche Kashkai, Tocol found its way blocked by tribesmen determined to stop the advance. A cavalry charge and RAF close air support finally forced

Map 5. Operations in North-West Frontier, 1935–1937.

the Wazir tribesmen back. While the road to Biche Kashkai appeared open, Tocol was now behind schedule. In order to link up with Razcol, the decision was made by the Tocol commander to continue the advance toward Biche Kashkai after dark. As Tocol moved forward in the darkness, tribesmen fired down on the column triggering a stampede by the pack mules laden with supplies. Approximately four miles from the perimeter camp at Biche Kashkai, Tocol was forced to hunker down in a defensive perimeter. During the night the situation grew so desperate for Tocol that the RAF was forced to parachute in four tons of supplies and ammunition to the beleaguered column at dawn. The next morning, Tocol managed to link up with Razcol at Biche Kashkai.[29]

On 27 November, however, a lack of supplies and the urgent need to evacuate casualties, forced both Tocol and Razcol to withdraw back to Mir Ali. The retreat greatly enhanced the power of the *Faqir* of Ipi. As historian Alan Warren pointed out; "The leadership displayed by the *Faqir* of Ipi was crucial to transforming the tribesmen's traditional desires for cultural and political autonomy and capacity for militancy, into active opposition. The *Faqir* also provided a charismatic focus for the tribesmen to identify with. Religion was used to define the enemy and to legitimize a military campaign. Religion was so closely allied to tribal culture that to some tribesmen a call to defend Islam had a clear political message."[30]

The tenacious resistance of the tribesmen had come as a shock to the British and Indian soldiers involved in the fighting. "The extent of the opposition offered to the columns was a surprise which exceeded all estimates;" wrote the author of the British official history. "In view of the amenability which the Tori *Khel* had shown previous to the operations, the only explanation seems to be that the *Faqir*'s propaganda had succeeded to an extent which had not been considered possible."[31] While the *Faqir* had managed to incite the population, the fact that the British telegraphed their intentions played a key role in the *Faqir's* victory. There was no surprise and no effort to secure a line of communication. As the British official history makes clear, the mission was undertaken with the expectation that it would be practically a peacetime operation. That is to say that any opposition would be slight only and the difficulties of reaching the day's objective would be those that might be expected normally in a column march."[32] Indeed, the Army of India had once again underestimated the Pashtun tribes and propelled the *Faqir* of Ipi into the spotlight. What had begun as a peacekeeping mission, now turned into a mission to punish the Tori *Khel* and track down and kill the *Faqir* of Ipi.

Reinforcements were immediately sent into North Waziristan. Light tanks, aircraft, and additional mountain batteries as well as engineers moved into position to support a new punitive expedition. While the new force was being assembled, British political officers met with various tribal *khels*. These *jirgas* convinced many tribal leaders to pull their fighters away from the *Faqir* of Ipi's *lashkar*. Although the *Faqir* lost many tribesmen, he gained more from Afghanistan as Pashtun tribesmen crossed the border to join the new holy war. Soon however, the additional manpower began to strain the primitive supply system of the *lashkar*.[33]

In early December, the new strike force advanced into the Khaisora Valley. This time they met with limited resistance as meager supplies and bad weather had forced many fighters to leave the *lashkar*. While the RAF conducted reduced bombing missions, the ground forces burned villages along the route belonging to Pashtun fighters. During the last week of December, British forces burned Biche Kashkai to the ground, forcing the *Faqir* of Ipi and about 850 fighters out of the Khaisora Valley. By January of 1937, the RAF had driven the *Faqir* and several hundred diehard fighters into caves outside of Arsal Kot. "Ultimately," wrote Alan Warren; "the lack of loot, supplies, and military success led to the dispersal of the insurgents."[34] As of mid-January of 1937, the Tori *Khel* Wazirs agreed to stop fighting. During this limited operation, 34 soldiers from the Army of India were killed and an additional 132 were wounded.

In the spring of 1937, after a short lull, violence once again flared in Waziristan. Far from beaten, the *Faqir* of Ipi emerged from his cavernous lair promoting a new *jihad*, while Wazir tribesmen launched new raids against the Hindu population along the Waziristan border. A limited bombing campaign by the RAF did little to stop the violence or placate the tribes. Permanent camps and outposts as well as permanent *piquets* throughout Waziristan, were frequently harassed by snipers while roving tribal gangs smashed telephone lines and other important infrastructure projects within Waziristan. The "Forward Policy" of occupying Waziristan and constructing a road network throughout the tribal areas was proving more of liability than an asset. Soldiers defending these outposts had to be supplied and maintaining the lengthy lines of communications proved a daunting task. The legendary John Masters, a young British officer serving in a Gurkha battalion at the time, recalled the difficulties of protecting the road networks in Waziristan;

> This was the hardest task [that] the Frontier offered and we did it three times a week. R.P. [Road Protection] was hard because every day we had to cover the same stretch of road and every day it became more difficult to obey the Cardinal Frontier principle of never doing the same thing in the same way twice running. We had to fight against fatigue and carelessness because someone was watching. Someone was always watching, someone with an inborn tactical sense, someone who missed nothing.[35]

Indeed, the tribesmen missed little. They were tactically proficient and always ready to attack an unsuspecting enemy. A case in point is the assault on the morning of the 9th of April in 1937. A convoy of 49 trucks carrying 72 men returning from leave and escorted by two automobiles, four armored cars, and two platoons of infantrymen proceeded up the road from Manzai and bound for Wana. Near the Shahur Tangi gorge, the convoy was ambushed by a force of Mahsud and Bhittani tribesmen led by the infamous Mahsud criminal, Khonia *Khel*. As the convoy rolled around the sharp curves of the gorge, the tribesmen unleashed a torrent of close range small arms fire. Drivers and passengers inside the trucks were riddled with bullets. The few who managed to get out of the vehicles, found little cover. To make matters worse, the armored cars were unable to elevate their machine guns high enough to engage the tribesmen on the high cliffs. The Mahsud and Bhittani fighters had chosen their ambush site well. "The tribesmen were in skillfully chosen positions on both sides of the road;" wrote the author of the British official history. "Concealed behind rocks and in catchment drains . . . and the tribesmen in many cases were completely protected from air attack under big overhanging slabs of rocks in front of which they had built walls."[36] The tribesmen even succeeded in shooting down a lone RAF aircraft that flew over the site of the ambush. During the course of the day and into the next morning, the fighting increased as reinforcements from Jandola and Wana rushed to rescue the survivors. By the time the fighting ended, the *lashkar* had disappeared into the hills, leaving 47 British and Indian soldiers dead and another 50 wounded.[37]

By the third week of April in 1937, British and Indian forces in Waziristan were confronting another powerful *lashkar* in Northern Waziristan. Restrictive bombing, negotiations, and limited punitive operations had all failed and the *Faqir* of Ipi once again returned, bringing with him approximately 3,000 fighters. On the 23rd of April, a force of nearly three brigades reinforced with light tanks and additional mountain artillery batteries advanced once again from Mir Ali into Khaisora Valley. A large amount of infantry was also employed to protect the vital lines of communication back to Mir Ali, while a wing from the RAF was placed under the direct control of the British ground commander.[38]

The ground forces at Biche Kashkai established a new base camp and *piquets* were positioned on the surrounding high ground. On the night of the 27th of April, Tori *Khel* tribesmen attacked the surrounding *piquets* with hand grenades and rifle fire while a larger force made a direct assault on the heavily defended camp at Biche Kashkai. This assault was easily beaten by machinegun and rifle fire from within the camp. Within days, the British commander was able to force a large section of the *lashkar* out into open ground where it was severely pummeled by aircraft, artillery and machinegun fire. While the *Faqir* of Ipi's *lashkar* suffered grievous losses, it was not destroyed. The tribesmen simply fell back into the Shaktu Valley where new fighters, including many Afghans, flocked to their banner forming more *lashkars*.[39]

In May, the British formed a new force christened the Waziristan Division or Wazdiv. This new division wasted little time in striking the *lashkars* in the Shaktu Valley. In a bold converging night movement across treacherous terrain, Wazdiv attacked the *lashkars* in the Shaktu region. Led by the Tochi Scouts, they surprised and overwhelmed the tribesmen who withdrew across the Sham Plain where they were cut down in large numbers by bombs and machinegun fire from RAF aircraft. Most of the Afghan fighters fled and were soon followed by other dejected tribesmen. As the British and Indian soldiers advanced toward the *Faqir* of Ipi's headquarters in the village of Arsal Kot, the RAF dropped 13,000 pounds of supplies. At the same time, ground forces secured the lines of communication back to Mir Ali. On the 28th of May, Arsal Kot was captured and destroyed without a fight. With the destruction of Arsal Kot, the Tori *Khel* tribesmen had had enough. Most of the fighters quit the field and returned to their homes, marking an end to large scale operations in Northern Waziristan. Once again however, the *Faqir* of Ipi slipped away.

From May until November in 1937, the British army continued to conduct small operations against hostile tribesmen in Waziristan. British and Indian soldiers built an additional 90 miles of road while continuing to fend off attacks by small groups of tribesmen. The operations had proven costly, with British and Indian forces sustaining almost 1,000 casualties during the campaign. By December, many of the brigades sent to reinforce Waziristan had returned to India. Interestingly, a light tank company was left in Waziristan to support the remaining soldiers in their garrison duties. According to one British historian; "The weight of firepower provided by machine guns, artillery, light tanks, and aircraft operating with Indian columns had proved highly effective against large concentrated *lashkars* in the opening phases of operations but conversely exacerbated the problem of bringing the elusive tribesmen to battle."[40] Indeed, as operations progressed and the tribesmen witnessed the destructive capabilities of these new weapon systems, they adjusted their tactics accordingly.[41]

As had been the case in past campaigns, the British sought to quickly inflict as much pain and punishment as possible on the errant tribesmen in order to establish calm. However, realizing the potential backlash of exceedingly harsh punitive measures, political officers sought to limit the damage inflicted on the tribes. It was perhaps, an early glimpse of today's COIN operations. Still, as British Army Officer John Masters pointed out; "We took few prisoners at any time and very few indeed if there was no political agent about."[42]

In the late 1930s, the British Army published *Frontier Warfare*, a new tactical manual for the North-West Frontier. The new handbook discussed the importance of converging attacks, night operations, *piqueting,* and strong firepower to cover withdrawals. Also identified as indispensable in frontier warfare against the Pashtuns, were the following: secrecy as regards intention, simplicity of plan, strict limitations of the objective through prior reconnaissance, mystification of the enemy, close control and supervision, and an ample margin of time.[43] While the new tactical manual provided solid lessons of past experiences, little had changed strategically on the North-West Frontier by the time the Second World War erupted in 1939. As T.R. Moreman asserted; "Despite repeated punitive campaigns and various attempts to pacify tribal territory, the now heavily armed transborder Pathans still remained fiercely independent and an insistent threat to the security of the settled areas. Apart from where roads had penetrated the hills, the main distinguishing characteristics and tactics of frontier warfare still remained essentially unchanged from those initially encountered in 1849 with large mobile columns reliant on pack transport protected by a ring of *piquets*."[44]

Even after the end of the Second World War, the *Faqir* of Ipi continued his war against the British from caves near the Afghan border. He would never be apprehended or killed by the British and died of old age in the 1960s.[45] When British rule ended in 1947, the problems associated with the Pashtuns of the North-West Frontier fell to the new Pakistani Government. That government chose at the time to remove all regular forces from the region. Today the Pakistani Army has returned to Waziristan and is confronted by a persistent and daunting adversary that closely resembles those cunning and resourceful enemy forces who opposed the British for much of the 20th century.

Notes

1. Quoted in T.R. Moreman, "'Passing It On:' The Army in India and Frontier Warfare, 1914–39" in *War and Society in Colonial India* edited by Kaushik Roy (New Delhi, India: Oxford University Press, 2006), 282.

2. Colonel J.P. Villiers-Stuart, *Letters of a Once Punjab Frontier Force Officer to His Nephew Giving His Ideas of Fighting on the North-West Frontier and in Afghanistan* (London: Sifton Praed & Co., Ltd., 1925), 25.

3. T.R. Moreman, *The Army in India and the Development of Frontier Warfare, 1849–1947* (London: Macmillan Press Ltd., 1998), 136.

4. *Manual of Operations on the North-West Frontier of India* (Calcutta, India: Government of India, Central Publication Branch, 1925), 3.

5. *Manual of Operations on the North-West Frontier of India*, 20.

6. *Manual of Operations on the North-West Frontier of India*, 25.

7. Villiers-Stuart, 24–25.

8. General Sir Andrew Skeen, *Passing It On: Short Talks on Tribal Fighting on The North-West Frontier Of India* (London: Gale and Polden, 1932), 62.

9. Quoted in T.R. Moreman, "'Passing It On:' The Army in India and Frontier Warfare, 1914–1939," 284.

10. T.R. Moreman, "'Passing It On:' The Army in India and Frontier Warfare, 1914–39," 285–286.

11. Charles Chenevix Trench, *The Frontier Scouts* (London, UK: Jonathan Cape, 1985), 129.

12. T.R. Moreman, "'Passing It On:' The Army in India and Frontier Warfare, 1914–1939," 285–286.

13. T.R. Moreman, "'Passing It On:' The Army in India and Frontier Warfare, 1914–1939," 287.

14. T.R. Moreman, "'Passing It On:' The Army in India and Frontier Warfare, 1914–1939," 289.

15. See *Tribal Fighting in NWFP* (Lahore, India: Vanguard Books, 2009).

16. Alan Warren, *Waziristan, the Faqir of Ipi and the Indian Army: The North-West Frontier Revolt of 1936–1937* (Oxford, UK: Oxford University Press, 2000), 65.

17. *Official History of Operations the North-West Frontier of India 1920–1935* (Sussex, UK: Published jointly by The Naval & Military Press Ltd. and The Imperial War Museum, n.d.), 192.

18. *Official History of Operations on the North-West Frontier of India 1920–1935*, 196.

19. *Official History of Operations on the North-West Frontier of India 1920–1935*, 196–197.

20. *Official History of Operations on the North-West Frontier 1920–1935*, 240–241.

21. *Official History of Operations on the North-West Frontier of India 1920–1935*, 241.

22. *Official History of Operations on the North-West Frontier of India 1920–1935*, 243;

23. Skeen, 20.

24. Quoted in T.R. Moreman, *The Army in India and the Development of Frontier Warfare, 1849–1947*, 152–153.

25. Swinson, 326.

26. Warren, 80–82; Swinson, 327.

27. Swinson, 327.

28. *Official History of Operations on the North-West Frontier of India 1936–1937* (Sussex, UK: Published jointly by The Naval & Military Press Ltd. and The Imperial War Museum, n.d.), 6–7.

29. *Official History of Operations on the North-West Frontier of India 1936–1937*, 7–8.

30. *Official History of Operations on the North-West Frontier of India 1936–1937*, 8; T.R. Moreman, *The Army in India and the Development of Frontier Warfare, 1849–1947*, 155.

31. Warren, 120.

32. *Official History of Operations on the North-West Frontier of India 1936–1937*, 15.

33. *Official History of Operations on the North-West Frontier of India 1936–1937*, 231.

34. T.R. Moreman, *The Army in India and the Development of Frontier Warfare, 1849–1947*, 156; Warren, 132.

35. Warren, 134–135.

36. Warren, 139, 144; T.R. Moreman, *The Army in India and the Development of Frontier Warfare, 1849–1947*, 156; John Masters, *Bugles and a Tiger: My Life in the Gurkhas* (London: Casell, 2002) quoted in T.R. Moreman, *The Army in India and the Development of Frontier Warfare, 1849–1947*, 158.

37. *Official History of Operations on the North-West Frontier of India 1936–1937*, 55.

38. Warren, 157.

39. T.R. Moreman, *The Army in India and the Development of Frontier Warfare, 1849–1947*, 159; Warren, 171–172.

40. T.R. Moreman, *The Army in India and the Development of Frontier Warfare, 1849–1947,* 159; Warren, 172.

41. T.R. Moreman, *The Army in India and the Development of Frontier Warfare, 1849–1947,* 165.

42. T.R. Moreman, *The Army in India and the Development of Frontier Warfare, 1849–1947,* 160–165.

43. Warren, 282.

44. *Official History of Operations on the North-West Frontier of India 1936–1937*, 234.

45. T.R. Moreman, *The Army in India and the Development of Frontier Warfare, 1849–1947,* 173.

46. T.R. Moreman, *The Army of India and the Development of Frontier Warfare 1849–1947*, 185; Warren, 259–260.

Conclusions

When the British finally withdrew from India in 1947, the Pashtun tribes of the North-West Frontier remained to a great extent, as they were in the 1840s. British efforts at pacification as well as punitive expeditions had failed to significantly alter the strategic situation. In the end, the introduction of modern weapons and continued tactical successes did little to fundamentally alter circumstances on the North-West Frontier. As they had been since the British arrived, the Pashtun population remained "an ever present danger" to those outside powers which sought control over the frontier area.[1] This assertion is underscored by the fact that in 2009, 60 years after the British departure from the region, the Pakistani government felt obligated to launch a military offensive against thousands of Pashtun insurgents in South Waziristan.[2]

In reviewing the pattern of military operations in the North-West Frontier over the last two centuries, it is clear that British objectives and practices differed from those of the Pakistani or US-led Coalition forces operating in the frontier region in the early 21st century. Most important is the fact that senior British military and political leaders were not interested in winning the hearts and minds of the Pashtun population on the North-West Frontier. Thus, British Imperial forces cannot be viewed as prosecuting campaigns of counterinsurgency in the region.

Then what can the US Army and its allies learn from the British experience on the North-West Frontier? Arguably, there are three fundamental insights offered by this historical experience. The first involves the set of problems associated with the training of an indigenous force. The significant tactical lessons from the British experience encompass the second, to include salient lessons on the use of key terrain and the integration of modern technology such as armored vehicles and aircraft. The third insight focuses on the importance of sustaining tactical doctrine and insights through the publication of both official and unofficial studies, manuals, and collections of lessons learned.

Like the US Army today, the British in the North-West Frontier trained and equipped thousands of native soldiers. Many of these soldiers served professionally and bravely in the British imperial ranks and certainly proved their worth in the mountains of the region. On at least two occasions however, trained Pashtun soldiers joined their fellow tribesmen in rebellions or holy wars against the British Army in India. In the 1897–1898 Pashtun revolts, tribesmen, both officers and soldiers, joined the *jihad* against the British Army in India. These former soldiers greatly inspired their comrades and communicated their considerable military knowledge to them. They also designed new tactics based of their familiarity with the British system. In the end, the British and Indian soldiers paid a heavy price in blood and equipment.

Once more during the campaigns of 1919–1920, a large number of Pashtuns soldiers trained by the British, joined forces with rebelling tribesmen. Many of these officers and soldiers had served in World War I and their insight and training allowed them to quickly form the *lashkars* into an imposing and tactically proficient force. As British historian Alan Warren pointed out, "Between 1900 and 1919 several thousand Wazirs, mainly Mahsuds, were recruited into the Indian Army and Frontier militias. Wazir junior officers learned how to control platoons and companies, and received an overview of battalion tactics."[3] Their training and skill undoubtedly helped bring about the enormous British and Indian losses incurred during this campaign. The British experience with training the indigenous population in the tactics and techniques of their own army cost the lives of many of their soldiers and proved to be a practice fraught with risk, however necessary it might have been. This is an important lesson that the US military should not overlook as it places more emphasis on building security forces in Afghanistan.

In the realm of tactical use of terrain, one of the most important lessons discovered by the British army in its campaigns against the Pashtuns was the importance of maintaining the high ground. Although it would appear to be a basic and straightforward tactical modus operandi, it was a practice sometimes overlooked by the British Army in India, often with deadly consequences. In order to guard against night attacks and deny the enemy the commanding terrain, trained and experienced frontier units almost always maintained *piquets,* or what today are called observation posts or combat outposts, on the high ground above their camps. Decades of lethal Pashtun surprise attacks in the rugged mountains of the North-West Frontier encouraged this tactical routine. "As soon as your battalion reaches camp, an officer reports for orders as to the camp *piquets*;" wrote General Andrew Skeen:

> If your C.O. [Commanding Officer] is wise, he will do what he can to speed up the occupation of these *piquets* . . . Meanwhile as many as can be spared from the rest of the company, with the company commander and good understudies to select the *piquet* sites, have gone up with full precautions and with ample tools and material, and there collect stones, fill sandbags, and build the walls.[4]

British units who failed to heed this advice were often ferociously battered by Pashtun tribesmen.

Piquets were sometimes employed by march columns to prevent ambush and surprise attacks by the Pashtuns. As the *Manual of Operations on the North-West Frontier of India* noted in 1925; "*Piquets* should be posted so as to deny to the enemy the most dangerous approaches and most important points within effective range of the route and to support one another. They must never withdraw without a definite order to do so."[5] Many times, a system of permanent *piquets* was also employed to guard lines of communication. This approach required plenty of soldiers and proved a slow and tedious process but was highly effective, nonetheless. Once again, British units that neglected to occupy the high ground were often severely punished by Pashtun tribes who rarely failed to exploit a mistake. Recent events in Afghanistan have shown that when Coalition forces have likewise failed to carefully place positions on key terrain, insurgents have been able to mount devastating attacks and inflict significant casualties.

As a modern industrialized power, the British Empire was able to introduce new technologies to the region beginning in the 20th century. Indeed, armored cars and light tanks offered important advantages on the North-West Frontier. When the terrain permitted their use, British and Indian soldiers fully exploited the armor, armaments, and mobility of these new weapons. "Armored cars are invaluable here;" wrote Skeen, "with command and protection, combined with fire power and speed, which gives them surprise properties of the greatest value."[6] The *Manual of Operations on the North-West Frontier of India*, published in 1925, made clear that the armored vehicles were "valuable for reconnaissance and pursuit, for the rapid support of a detachment, and for escorting motor convoys."[7] The *Official History of Operations on the North-West Frontier of India 1920–1935*, also pointed out,"Armoured troops, owing to their invulnerability to rifle fire and to the absence of hostile artillery or aircraft can be of great value in Frontier Warfare."[8] The *Official History* also stated that through the use of tanks; "opposition to a direct advance by our infantry was reduced."[9] Indeed, during the campaigns, light tanks proved highly successful in neutralizing enemy small arms fire, threatening the flanks and rear of the *lashkars,* and assisting in the placement and withdrawal of infantry *piquets.*[10]

While the insurgent enemy in Afghanistan is now equipped with modern anti-tank weapons and a profusion of improvised explosive devices (IEDs), it would be incorrect to assume that armored vehicles and tanks have no place in current operations. The Canadian Army's experience with tanks in Afghanistan from 2006 to 2007, to a great extent, mirrors that of the British on the North-West Frontier. According to Canadian Major Trevor Cadieu, tanks and other armored vehicles; "have better protected our dismounted infantry soldiers in Southern Afghanistan, allowing them to close with and destroy a fanatical and determined enemy in extremely complex terrain."[11] Cadieu also confirmed the psychological importance of tanks in Afghanistan, contending that; "Numerous signal and human intelligence (HUMINT) reports confirm that lower-level Taliban fighters are terrified of the tanks and their ability to manoeuvre and they are often reluctant to attack coalition forces equipped with integral armoured assets."[12] British light tanks produce the same effects on the Pashtun tribesmen of the North-West Frontier. The US military in 2009 began introducing Stryker Combat Vehicles to combat operations in Afghanistan. US commanders and planners should consider the recent Canadian experience as well as the British experience from the previous century in their considerations of how to use these vehicles.

Aircraft also became increasingly important in British operations in the North-West Frontier. In his recent paper *Britain & the North-West Frontier: Strategy, Tactics and Lessons*, Jules Stewart writes; "From the early years of the 20th century, air power came to play a significant role in combating tribal insurgents."[13] Indeed, the Royal Air Force performed a number of important missions and closely supported the British Army ground operations. As T.R. Moreman pointed out; "The RAF assisted the army with supporting *piquets*, assisting withdrawals, directing artillery fire, communicating between advance and rear guards, and supplying photographic intelligence."[14] The RAF also operated independently, often carrying out punitive attacks on Pashtun tribesmen and their livestock in an effort to bring the wayward tribesmen to terms. However, British political officers frequently forced the RAF to limit these measures, cognizant of the fact that this type of activity was counterproductive and would only broaden the conflict. This serves as a critical caution for both the US Army and its allies.

Perhaps the best observation regarding the use of air power against the Pashtuns on the North-West Frontier however, came from British General Sir Andrew Skeen; "My own view is that these people [the Pashtun tribes] are really so invulnerable in their miserable property and in their persons save from accurate close range use of ground weapons and are moreover so scattered and so adept at cover and concealment that I doubt whether any tribe that has the will to resist, will ever be coerced by air power alone."[15] While written nearly 80 years ago and before the advent of precision-guided weapons and unmanned aerial vehicles, Skeen's insight on the use of air power against the Pashtun tribes in the region remains a useful caveat about the limits of modern technology.

The broadest, and perhaps most durable, insight concerns the manner in which military institutions learn and develop. As documented in this study, a host of British officers produced both official and unofficial tactical studies and manuals during the nearly one hundred years of conflict on the North-West Frontier. From Captain Charles Farquhar Trower's *Hints on Irregular Cavalry*, published in 1845, to General Sir Andrew Skeen's *Passing It On*, published in the late 1930s, British officers sought to convey their knowledge and experience in unofficial publications designed to assist fellow officers and soldiers in conducting operations on the North-West Frontier. Official British army manuals also attempted to pass on this same understanding of mountain warfare and the complexities of confronting the Pashtun tribes. For the most part, these authors succeeded in educating the soldiers who would conduct punitive operations against the tribes. However, when British senior commanders failed to disseminate this doctrine to the regular forces or minimized frontier fighting manuals by combining them with more standardized field service regulations, lessons were lost and problems often followed. Conducting combat operations against the Pashtuns in the mountainous terrain of the North-West Frontier required specialized training for soldiers as well as specific training manuals. By the late 1930s and 1940s, the British army had learned these lessons well and provided their soldiers with the required frontier manuals as well as instructive official histories of past campaigns. In its collection and dissemination of lessons learned in Afghanistan and publication of studies like the present volume, the US Army has wisely chosen to emulate this practice and should continue to do so into the future.

Notes

1. Lieutenant Colonel C.E. Bruce, *Waziristan: The Problems of the North-West Frontiers of India and Their Solutions* (Aldershot, Gale & Polden, Ltd., 1938), vii.

2. Ishtiaq Mahsud and Nahal Toosi, "Pakistan attacks militant bases," *The Kansas City Star*, 18 October 2009.

3. Alan Warren, *Waziristan, the Faqir of Ipi and the Indian Army: The North-West Frontier Revolt of 1936–1937* (Oxford, UK: Oxford University Press, 2000), 280.

4. General Sir Andrew Skeen, *Passing It On: Short Talks on Tribal Fighting on the North-West Frontier of India* (London: Gale and Polden, 1932), 71.

5. *Manual of Operations on the North-West Frontier of India* (Calcutta, India: Government of India, Central Publication Branch, 1925), 21–22.

6. Skeen, 99, 116.

7. *Manual of Operations on the North-West Frontier of India*, 14

8. *Official History of Operations on the North-West Frontier of India 1920–1935* (Sussex, UK: Published jointly by The Naval & Military Press Ltd. and The Imperial War Museum, n.d.), 243.

9. *Official History of Operations on the North-West Frontier of India 1920–1935*, 243.

10. *Official History of Operations on the North-West Frontier of India 1920–1935*, 243.

11. Major Trevor Cadieu, "Canadian Armour in Afghanistan," *Canadian Army Journal*, Vol. 10, No. 4 (Winter 2008), 5.

12. Cadieu, 21.

13. Jules Stewart, *Britain & the North-West Frontier: Strategy, Tactics and Lessons* (Washington, DC: The Jamestown Foundation, 2009), 6.

14. T.R. Moreman, *The Army of India and the Development of Frontier Warfare* (London: Macmillan Press Ltd., 1998), 131.

15. Skeen, 21–22.

Select Glossary of Afghan Tribal Terms

faqir	a holy man
ghazi	a Muslim who devotes his life to killing an infidel or fighting unbelievers
jezail	Pashtun long musket
jirga	a gathering of tribal representatives or elders
khassadar	a tribal levy who, in return for certain responsibilities, receives pay from the government
khel	tribal sub-group or kinship group
lashkar	a tribal army (not usually applied to less than 200 men)
malik	a tribal representative or elder
mullah	a religious teacher or leader
Pashtunwali	unwritten Pashtun code of conduct; "the way of the Pashtun"
sangar	a stone breastwork

Bibliography

Books

A Dictionary of the Pathan Tribes in the North-West Frontier of India. Delhi, India: Mittal Publications, 1983.

Allen, Charles. *God's Terrorists: The Wahhabi Cult and the Hidden Roots of Modern Jihad*. Cambridge, MA: Da Capo Press, 2006.

_____. *Soldier Sahibs: The Daring Adventurers Who Tamed India's North-West Frontier*. New York: Carroll & Graf Publishers, Inc., 2000.

Barbero, Alessandro. *The Battle: A New History of Waterloo*, trans. John Cullen. New York: Walker & Company, 2003.

Barthorp, Michael. *Afghan Wars and the North-West Frontier 1839–1947*. London: Cassell, 1982.

Bruce, Lieutenant Colonel C.E. *Waziristan 1936-1937: The Problems of the North-West Frontiers of India and Their Solutions*. Aldershot, UK: Gale & Polden, Ltd., Wellington Works, 1938.

Churchill, Winston. *The Story of The Malakand Field Force: An Episode of Frontier War*. New York: W.W. Norton & Company, 1990.

Dichter, David. *The North-West Frontier of West Pakistan: A Study in Regional Geography*. Oxford, UK: Clarendon Press, 1967.

Enriquez, C.M. *The Pathan Borderland: A consecutive account of the country and people on and beyond the Indian frontier from Chitral to Dera Ismail Khan*. Calcutta and Simla, India: Thacker, Spink & Co., 1921.

Fincastle, The Viscount and Eliott-Lockhart, P.C. *A Frontier Campaign: A Narrative of the Operations of the Malakand and Buner Field Forces, 1897–1898*. London: Methuen & Co., 1898.

Heathcote, T.A. *The Afghan Wars 1839–1919*. Kent, UK: Spellmount, 2003.

_____. *The Indian Army: The Garrison of British Imperial India, 1822–1922*. New York: Hippocrene Books, 1974.

Kaplan, Robert D. *Soldiers of God: With Islamic Warriors in Afghanistan and Pakistan*. New York: Vintage Departures, 2001.

Masters, John. *Bugles and a Tiger: My Life in the Gurkhas*. London: Casell, 2002.

Mazumder, Rajit K. *The Indian Army and the Making of Punjab*. Delhi, India: Permanent Black, 2003.

Metcalf, Barbara D. and Thomas R. Metcalf. *A Concise History of Modern India*. Second edition. Cambridge, UK: Cambridge University Press, 2006.

Miller, Charles. *Khyber: British India's North-West Frontier The Story of an Imperial Migraine*. New York: Macmillan, 1977.

Mills, Woosnam. *Pathan Revolts in North-West India*. Lahore, India: Sang-E-Meel Publications, 1979.

Mohmand, Sher Muhammad. *The Pathan Customs*. Peshawar, Pakistan: n.d., 2003.

Molesworth, Lieutenant General G.N. *Afghanistan 1919: An Account of Operations in the Third Afghan War*. New York: Asia Publishing House, 1962.

Moore, Geoffrey, *"Just as Good as the Rest:"A British Battalion in the Faqir of Ipi's War on the Indian N.W.F. 1936–37.* Huntington: privately published, 1979.

Moreman, T.R. *The Army in India and the Development of Frontier Warfare, 1849–1947.* London: Macmillan Press Ltd., 1998.

_____. "'The Greatest Training Ground in the World:' The Army in India and the North-West Frontier 1901–1947." In *A Military History of India and South Asia from the East India Company to the Nuclear Era* edited by Daniel P. Marston and Chandar S. Sundaram. Westport, CT: Praeger Security International, 2007.

_____. "'Passing It On:'" The Army in India and Frontier Warfare, 1914–39." In *War and Society in Colonial India* edited by Kaushik Roy. Oxford, UK: Oxford University Press, 2006.

Mukulika, Banerjee. *The Pathan Unarmed: Opposition & Memory in the North-West Frontier.* Karachi, Pakistan: Oxford University Press, 2000.

Nevill, Captain H.L. *Campaigns on the North-West Frontier.* Nashville, TN: The Battery Press, 1912.

North, Lieutenant Colonel R.I.A. *The Literature of the North-West Frontier of India: A Select Bibliography.* N.p., 1946.

Obhrai, Diwan Chand. *The Evolution of the North-West Frontier Province: A Survey of the History and Constitutional Development of N.W.F. Province in India.* Peshawar, Pakistan: Saeed Book Bank & Subscription Agency, 1983.

Pennell, Alice M. *Pennell of the Afghan Frontier: The Life of Theodore Leighton Pennell.* London: Seeley, Service & Co. Ltd., 1914.

Robson, Brian. *Crisis on the Frontier: The Third Afghan War and the Campaign in Waziristan 1919–1920.* Staplehurst, UK: Spellmount, 2004.

Skeen, General Sir Andrew. *Passing It On: Short Talks on Tribal Fighting on the North-West Frontier of India.* London: Gale and Polden, 1932.

Stewart, Jules. *Britain & the North-West Frontier: Strategy, Tactics And Lessons.* Washington, DC: The Jamestown Foundation, 2009.

_____. *The Khyber Rifles: From the British Raj to Al Qaeda.* Phoenix Mill, UK: Sutton Publishing Ltd., 2005.

Story of the North-West Frontier Province. Peshawar, Pakistan: Manager, Government Printing and Stationary Office North-West Frontier Province, 1930.

Swinson, Arthur. *North-West Frontier: People and Events, 1839–1947.* New York: Frederick A. Praeger, Publishers, 1967.

The Risings on the North-West Frontier. Allahabad, India: Printed and Published at the Pioneer Press, 1898.

Torrens-Spence, Johnny. *Historic Battlefields of Pakistan.* Oxford, UK: Oxford University Press, 2006.

Trench, Charles Chenevix. *The Frontier Scouts.* London: Jonathan Cape, 1985.

Trower, Captain Charles Farquhar. *Hints on Irregular Cavalry, Its Conformation, Management and Use in Both a Military and Political Point of View.* Calcutta, India: W. Thacker and Co., 1845.

Villiers-Stuart, Colonel J.P. *Letters of a Once Punjab Frontier Force Officer to His Nephew: Giving His Ideas on Fighting on the North-West Frontier and in Afghanistan*. London: Sifton Praed & Co. Ltd., 1925.

Waller, John H. *Beyond The Khyber Pass: The Road to British Disaster in the First Afghan War*. New York: Random House, 1990.

Warren, Alan. *Waziristan, the Faqir of Ipi and the Indian Army: The North-West Frontier Revolt of 1936–1937*. Oxford, UK: Oxford University Press, 2000.

de Watteville, H. *Waziristan, 1919–1920*. Campaigns and Their Lessons Series. London: Constable and Co. Ltd., 1925.

Woods, Frederick, ed. *Young Winston's Wars: The Original Dispatches of Winston S. Churchill War Correspondent 1897–1900*. London: Leo Cooper Ltd., 1972.

Younghusband, G.J. *Indian Frontier Warfare*. London: Kegan Paul, Trench, Trubner & Co., Ltd., 1898.

Internet Sources

Tharoor, Ishaan. "The Original Insurgent." *Time*. 19 April 2007. http://www.time.com/time/magazine/article/0,9171,1612380,00.html (accessed 15 June 2009).

Newspapers

Ahmed, Khaled. "The Curse of Retired Generals." *Daily Times*, 9 September 2003. http://www.dailytimes.com.pk/default.asp?page=story_9-9-2003_pg3_6 (accessed 1 June 2009).

Mahsud, Ishtiaq and Nahal Toosi. "Pakistan attacks militant bases." *The Kansas City Star*. Kansas City, MO: 18 October, 2009.

"Restoration of Peace for FATA Uplift Urged." *Business Recorder,* 13 March 2008. http://www.brecorder.com/index.php?show=&&id=708259&currPageNo=6&query=&search=&term=&supDate= (accessed 17 June 2009).

Rose, David. "Hunting the Taliban in the footsteps of Winston Churchill: On the lawless battlefields nothing has changed in a century." *Daily Mail Online*, 20 June 2009. http://www.dailymail.co.uk/news/worldnews/article-1194352/Hunting-Taliban-footsteps-Winston-Churchill.html (accessed 21 June 2009).

Sitaraman, Ganesh. "The Land of 10,000 Wars." *The New York Times*, 17 August 2009.

Official Reports

General Report on the Administration of the Punjab for the Years 1849-1850 and 1850-1851. London: Printed for the Court of Directors of the East India Company, 1854.

Official History of Operations the North-West Frontier of India 1920–1935. Sussex, UK: Published jointly by The Naval & Military Press Ltd. and The Imperial War Museum, n.d.

Official History of Operations on the North-West Frontier of India 1936–1937.
Sussex, UK: Published jointly by The Naval & Military Press Ltd. and
The Imperial War Museum, n.d.

Published Articles

Cadieu, Major Trevor. "Canadian Armour in Afghanistan." *Canadian Army
Journal*, Vol. 10, No. 4 (Winter 2008).

Hauner, Milan. "One Man against the Empire: The *Faqir* of Ipi and the British in
Central Asia on the Eve of and during the Second World War." *Journal of
Contemporary History*, Vol. 16, No. 1 (January 1981).

Johnson, Thomas H. and M. Chris Mason. "No Sign until the Burst of Fire:
Understanding the Pakistan-Afghanistan Frontier." *International
Security*, Vol. 32, No. 4 (Spring 2008).

Muspratt, Colonel S.F. "Military Situation on the North-West Frontier of India,"
Aldershot Military Society, CXX. London: Hugh Rees, 1922.

Strausz-Hupe, Robert. "The Anglo-Afghan War of 1919." *Military Affairs*, Vol. 7,
No. 2 (Summer 1943).

Training Manuals

Manual of Operations on the North-West Frontier of India. Calcutta, India:
Government of India, Central Publication Branch, 1925.

About the Author

Matt M. Matthews joined the Combat Studies Institute (CSI) in July 2005. For 16 years he was a member of the World Class Opposing Forces (OPFOR) of the Battle Command Training Program (BCPT) at Fort Leavenworth, Kansas. Enlisting in the Army at age 17, he served in the light infantry from 1977 to 1981. Mr. Matthews also served as a Cavalry officer in the US Army Reserve from 1983 to 1986 and as an Armor Officer in the Kansas Army National Guard from 1986 to 1991. He graduated from Kansas State University in 1986 with a BS in History and continued his graduate studies there. Mr. Matthews is the author of several CSI Press publications including *The Posse Comitatus Act* and *The United States Army: A Historical Perspective, Operation AL FAJR: A Study in Army and Marine Corps Joint Operations, The US Army on the Mexican Border: A Historical Perspective*, and *We Were Caught Unprepared: The 2006 Hezbollah-Israeli War*. He also contributed the chapter titled "Hard Lessons Learned A Comparison of the 2006 Hezbollah-Israeli War and Operation CAST LEAD: A Historical Overview" in the CSI publication *Back To Basics: A Study of the Second Lebanon War and Operation CAST LEAD*.

Matt has coauthored numerous scholarly articles on the Civil War in the Trans-Mississippi with Kip Lindberg, including "Shot All to Pieces: The Battle of Lone Jack," "To Play a Bold Game: The Battle of Honey Springs," "Better Off in Hell: The Evolution of the Kansas Red Legs", and "It Haunts Me Night and Day: The Baxter Springs Massacre." Mr. Matthews is a frequent speaker at Civil War Roundtables and recently appeared on the History Channel as a historian for Bill Kurtis' Investigating History program. Mr. Matthews is a former mayor of Ottawa, Kansas. He is currently writing a biography of Kansas Civil War General James G. Blunt and a book on the Kansas Red Legs.